LE CHÂTEAU

A VERY FRENCH AFFAIR

LE CHÂTEAU

A VERY FRENCH AFFAIR

NICK HAMPTON

ORiGiN™ IMPRiNT

First published in Australia in 2021
by ORiGiN™ IMPRiNT
ABN 46 111 477 895
originimprint.com

A catalogue record for this book is available from the National Library of Australia

Hampton, Nick, author.
Le Château: A Very French Affair
ISBN: 978-0-6485874-9-1

Cover design by Amber Quin
Cover drawing by Bel Ford
Editing by Gary Martin
Typesetting by Amber Quin

ORiGiN™ IMPRiNT
PO Box 1235
QVB Post Office
NSW 1230 Australia
originimprint.com

Nick Hampton had a distinguished international career as a music industry executive and managing director in London, Europe, the USA and Australia. He was involved with Petula Clark, Elton John, The Kinks, Tony Hatch, Jackie Trent, Donovan, Sandie Shaw, Johnny Cash, Andy Williams, Tony Bennett, Vera Lynn, Slim Dusty, Neil Finn, Jimmy Barnes and other leading artists. Music also brought him into contact with legendary business figures such as Lew Grade, Dick James, Clive Davis and Ted Albert, who was pivotal in AC/DC's breakthrough. *Le Château: A Very French Affair* is his first novel. He lives in retirement with his wife in the south of France.

Also by Nick Hampton

NICK OF TIME: MY LIFE AND CAREER,
ALL ON THE RECORD

I dedicate this book to Jean, my children and to
"France: the first love of my life."

1.

THE DREAM

THEY had all fallen in love the moment they saw her. Although she was more than four hundred years old and ravaged by the elements there was an air of peace about her and a tranquillity that came from seeing seasons – and occupants – come and go.

The late August sun shone on a face that was totally shuttered. Shadows from the tall plane trees in the park flickered across it, making it seem as if she was in a restful sleep, dreaming perhaps of those other, more stressful times, when the countryside had been pulled apart by religious and civil wars and occupation by foreign powers.

An estate agent was waiting for them by the front door and he was not happy, as he resented having to work on a day when most of France was on holiday. But he greeted them cordially and extended his hand.

"Bonjour, *Mesdames et Messieurs*. You will excuse my poor English but I am here to show you Le Château du Moulin. Please call me Tomas."

Inside, Tomas opened the shutters and light flooded into the cool interior. The two-storey building was about one hundred metres wide, with wings at each end that formed a shallow forecourt. Built of light grey stone blocks nearly sixty centimetres in depth, the house was pierced at regular intervals by windows three metres high and a generous width. A small circular tower graced the south-eastern corner, and both the tower and residence were roofed with the dark grey slate so typical of the region.

Behind the northern end of the château stood the historic building that gave it its name: a twelfth-century millhouse with a water-wheel still projecting over the dried-up channel that once fed it from the sparkling river flowing by, a tributary of the Tarn that had its source high in the Massif Central region in the middle of southern France.

The central part of the château's ground floor contained inter-connected rectangular rooms which overlooked the back garden facing north-east and sloping gently towards the river and a long line of poplars. The inspection party walked from room to room, silently admiring the high ceilings, nearly four metres, and the generous french doors and windows. As they progressed, the slumbering house seemed to be stirring itself into a watching wakefulness.

Tomas led them up the beautiful curving staircase to a broad landing like a balcony which led left and right into the bedrooms. These were pretty awful: different shapes and sizes, some accessed by a narrow corridor, some through connecting doors. There were twelve in all, and two large bathrooms with attached toilets at either end of the building.

"This would take some planning," said Mark. It was the first time anybody had spoken since they walked in.

The four visitors plus Tomas spent over an hour wandering through the château and the spacious gardens. They inspected the millhouse and peered over a hedge separating this property from the neighbouring farm, which was still occupied and had once been part of a much bigger property that included the château before being legally hived off.

The gardens in front of the château were a picture of formality. Set in freshly clipped lawns, half-circles of rose beds and flowering cherry trees surrounded a stone pond twenty metres in diameter which had a central fountain in the shape of a naked nymph and six small water jets. Beyond the gardens, plane trees, oaks, cedars and an assortment of pines, bushes and smaller trees grew in profusion along the laneway to a verdant swathe of parkland. The gardens and the park were bordered on one side by a two hundred-metre driveway and on the other side by the hedge which rather haphazardly designated the boundary between the château and the farm.

The Château du Moulin sat on ten hectares of land where animals once grazed amid the crop fields. But the proprietors had fallen on hard times, the years of being a productive farm were long gone, and the property had been on the market for eighteen months without attracting a serious offer.

As they went back inside, taking photographs with their iPhones, Toby drew a sketch of the château's ground floor, where a large windowless room had once been used for the storage of wine and other provisions, while the others had a last look around.

The inspection ended at four p.m. and Tomas closed the shutters as the others walked outside.

"Tomas," said Mark, "I speak I'm sure for all of us when I say that we are most grateful to you for spending your Friday afternoon with us. It is a fascinating house and perhaps what we are looking for. We are now going on to spend the night in Toulouse before catching the train to Paris and then the Eurostar back home to London, so we shall have time to discuss everything. I will contact you on Monday. Thank you again and *au revoir.*"

And with that they drove slowly through the château's huge wrought-iron gates to the narrow road winding between fields where wheat had recently been harvested and sunflowers were hanging down in the heat, and on to Toulouse.

***

They were staying at the Grand Hotel Opera, a beautiful old building with refurbished suites near Le Capitole, which housed the Hotel de Ville as well as art galleries, and had a history dating back several centuries. After checking in they went for dinner at Le Bibent, just across the main square. Owned and run by master chef Christian Constant, it was a beautiful restaurant decorated in the style of the Belle Époque, with ornate mirrors framed in gold-leaf, and a sumptuous menu. Toby went for the *cassoulet* while the others chose various fish dishes as the first bottle of wine was poured.

"Okay, around the table," Mark said, "starting with Jenny."

"Couldn't help but love it," Jenny said. "Toby and I adored the setting, the park, the views, everything. But there's a lot of work to be done. It didn't look as if the plumbing had been touched for centuries. And where was the kitchen?"

Toby broke in.

"We think the main point in its favour is the location, but could it be converted or restored to a state that'd meet what we're looking for?"

"And what exactly is that?" asked Mark.

"A place where we can all live, but not be on top of each other. Where we can accommodate and entertain friends together, and separately when we want to. When Pru and Jenny's parents visit we shouldn't all feel obliged to have three meals with them every day. We've got two kids and the first grandchild is on the way, and Chris has two already. We all love being together, we do it all the time, but we need our own space too."

"You're right," Pru responded. "Mark and I have discussed that, and we think we just might be able to make it work at the château. Mark has a suggestion to make."

"Well, we seem to be agreed on our objectives," he said. "Next, I seem to remember, come the strategies."

"That's our planner speaking," said Toby, and everyone laughed and relaxed.

"Thanks, Toby," Mark replied. "I'm not sure if that was a vote of confidence or not but I'll continue. The château has about fifteen hundred square metres on each floor. Take out the coldroom and the hall with the staircase and landing and you're probably left with well over two thousand square metres of renewable space all up. I don't imagine we can do much with the exterior – Tomas told us it was heritage-listed – but I reckon we could make something spectacular of the ground floor, and the top floor could be completely remodelled. Probably all we need is inspiration, a great designer, plenty of time, and a shitload of money."

"Well, thanks mostly to Toby and his recommendations on what and when to short-sell, we made quite a bit during the GFC," said Pru, "so that shouldn't be a worry. We're in a good position."

"Thanks, Pru, but I don't think we should make too much of that," Toby suggested. "We bankers are not exactly the flavour of the month at the moment and that's probably as true here as anywhere else in the world."

They enjoyed their dinner over more banter and headed off for an early night.

After returning the hire car they had breakfast the next morning and headed to the train station. Once settled in their seats they were overtaken by thinking about the holiday they had just enjoyed together. They had, not for the first time, rented a house for two weeks at Cap d'Antibes and spent several days before and after touring the south and south-western parts of France, looking at houses for sale on various websites. This was a passion they had shared for years, and as they got to know the countryside better they came to the conclusion that the south-west was best for them. In particular they were favouring the region of the Midi-Pyrenées. "Not as many bloody English for a start," Pru declared. That is how they had come to inspect Le Château du Moulin, tucked away in the quiet village of Saint Audan – and Pru could have added "less bloody expensive too".

They exchanged a lot of euros for four small espressos and started reviewing yesterday's experience, Jenny first.

"We've all got jobs and nice homes in London but we're all planning to retire in the next few years, so we don't have to hurry this project. Do we think the château could be a goer?"

Pru joined in. "Mark has some thoughts, but he says no commitment until we're satisfied that we could turn it into a wonderful holiday home. And a long-term home for our retirement if that's what we want when the time comes."

"Do you remember my friend Clive Stevens?" Mark asked. "He's still a partner in Holmes and Stevens, the interior designers. Mostly works on major projects like new hotels in Dubai and art galleries. I think he's played a minor role in the new one funded by the Louis Vuitton Foundation in the Bois de Boulogne. But I know he loves playing with old ruins, as he calls it. I propose that I contact him and see if he could get involved in working out a design for the château, and checking that it's not about to slip into an underground fracking hole."

They all agreed, and before they reached Calais, Mark phoned Clive and arranged a lunch meeting for the next Tuesday at the Groucho Club, a private club in Soho with members mostly drawn from publishing, entertainment, the media and the arts.

***

Mark had signed in his guest, so Clive was shown up to the bar when he arrived at the club just after one o'clock.

"What a great place, Mark. My first time here, so you must tell me all about it."

They went straight to their table for pre-lunch drinks and Clive was fascinated by the drawings of celebrities that filled the walls.

"How come you're a member here?" he asked.

"A real bit of luck," Mark replied. "When I was the MD at Solway Records I was asked to join an industry panel looking at how we could use the internet to benefit songwriters, artists and recording companies. Apple iTunes filled a bit of the gap initially, but we had to find other ways of reducing illegal downloads. So I got to know a lot of those concerned, including probably the biggest-earning songwriter in England, and he put me up for membership even though I didn't really fit the criteria. It's a great place and the food isn't half bad either. Let's order."

"So why the invitation?" Clive asked. "It's ages since I last saw you and then, right out of the blue, an urgent-sounding request to join you for lunch. Is everything okay?"

"Everything's fine," Mark said, launching into a rundown on the visit to the château and outlining what he was asking him to do.

Clive nodded as he got the broad picture.

"But so that I am aware of the dynamics and the relationships of all those concerned, perhaps you could give me some background. For instance, how did you get to know Toby?"

"We were at school together," Mark said, "but I'm a couple of years older and I don't remember Toby from those days. Then a few years later we happened to be dating two sisters, Pru and Jenny, who are now our wives. We used to go out as a foursome, I discovered Toby played golf, and so it went. Toby was my best man and I was his two years later. We get on really well, despite or perhaps because of being so different. Toby is almost a geek. Incredibly astute at maths. He designed lots of the algorithms his bank uses to predict the probability of currency movements and the price of derivatives. I only know this because he's told me, but it's no secret that he's on a bonus which makes most of the successful traders sound under-rewarded. He also plays the markets himself. He's loaded, Clive. I've done pretty nicely from promoting and managing bands in my early days, but our Toby is the big success story and he's helped us make some nice little profits too. We don't talk too much about that though."

Mark took another sip of the excellent claret accompanying his filet mignon.

"Pru is the older sister by about three years and she runs a charity that's closely linked to the old music industry, as we call it, the Golden Clef Music Therapy Centre. It provides interactive music therapy to help all sorts of people, from very young kids with autism up to seniors with dementia. Not so much for cures, but to improve the quality of their life and the lives of their carers. She's very dedicated and loves the daily challenges."

"And Jenny?" Clive said.

"Jenny started off as a primary school teacher and became head of a big school in Wandsworth, but by the time she got to fifty she was worn out and gave it up. Now she's in charge of a unit in the Department of Education which tries to look after kids with special needs. Even more exhausting if you ask me. The girls' parents are in their eighties and still pretty active. He was a High Court judge, she stayed home and raised three kids – there's a brother in between, Charles. We both have children and grandchildren, just, and lots of friends who love coming to visit us in France. That's it in a nutshell."

"So ideally," said Clive, "you are looking to have a place with separate living space but communal areas where you can entertain, and spare rooms for guests. Also where you can enjoy outdoor entertaining, gardens, a swimming pool, etcetera? Does that sound about right?"

"It does, Clive."

"Okay. Let's drink to your château and I'll see what I can do."

On the following Friday, Mark, Clive and one of his young assistants flew to Toulouse, hired a car and met Tomas, who gave them the keys to the Château du Moulin for the weekend.

The assistant, a pretty girl called Linda, took dozens of photos inside and out and downloaded them onto her iPad. She and Clive had apps which enabled them to measure and visually record each space, so by Saturday evening they had assembled enough data for Clive to draw up a complete plan of the interior. They also took videos of the external façades and the grounds.

"That's it," Clive said as they boarded their plane home. "Give me ten days and I'll have something for you. It's already beginning to come together, but there's a lot of work to do with computer designing before I can tell you whether we can make your dream come true."

＊＊＊

Two weeks later they all reassembled in the big dining room of Mark and Pru's house in Hampstead. Clive and Linda brought drawings as well as audiovisual material to support their design concepts.

"First of all, a tour of the garden and a look at the outside of the house," Clive said. He demonstrated his preference for a terrace with an entertaining and barbecue area located to function with the installation of the new kitchen. The location and dimensions of a swimming pool were also proposed, without dissent. Then the tour went indoors.

"I decided to incorporate the millhouse into my plan," he explained, "for two reasons. Firstly, it allows for a separate entrance to what would become one of two self-contained areas. It also reduces the impact of families and guests all using the same main staircase, although I'll come back to that later. Secondly, because the millhouse will have its own water and heating facilities, it could be used independently of the main house. It is virtually what the French call a *gite*, with two bedrooms, one bathroom upstairs and a living room, as well as an American kitchen. Roughly sixty square metres all up over two levels, plenty of living space."

Clive continued with the presentation.

"Now we are back in the château. The first thing to show you is how I would build the main kitchen. It's at the western end of the building and it incorporates the existing coolroom. It's forty square metres, large enough to put in two of almost everything: refrigerators, ovens, hotplates and sinks, plus lots of work surfaces in the central island, so you could cater for a big number of people. From there we're in the dining room, which is roomy enough for a very large table as well as plenty of storage space for crockery and glassware. And this design has direct access from both the kitchen and the dining room to the outside entertaining area."

The demonstration went on through the main hall and three

other ground-floor rooms, the last of which was the drawing room which had a huge open fireplace.

"I just had to keep that fireplace," Clive said. "And Pru, I know you want to have a good space for a piano. My recommendation would be to put it in the entrance hall. You could use the stairs and, rather interestingly I think, the balcony for performers on other instruments as well as vocalists, and have seating for at least sixty guests. You could give some lovely concerts there, but I'm not an expert on acoustics, so we would have to check the sound quality."

"That's a great idea, Clive. I like it," Pru said.

Clive moved on to the upstairs blueprint.

"I've used the western end of the château to create a self-contained flat with two bedrooms, a living room and a bathroom, but no kitchen. I'm proposing to compensate for that by putting in this small secondary staircase which goes down directly to the main kitchen. But if that's not acceptable I could lose one of the guest rooms and put a kitchen in the flat. That would bring the number of guest rooms down to six, each with an ensuite. So . . . thoughts? Comments?"

The resulting debate was lengthy but positive. Mark and Toby let the girls run with it first. They were pretty happy and avoided an instant decision on which family would have the *gite* and which one the flat; both seemed almost equally attractive. Then Mark stepped in.

"And how much are we looking at, Clive?"

"Well, there's quite a lot of structural work to do on the upper floor, but I've pretty much reutilised what's downstairs. I would seriously suggest replacing all the windows and french doors with new ones, double-glazed. It'll save you heaps on heating in the long run. I'd also strip out the wiring and plumbing and start from scratch. Then there's the millhouse, which will be quite a task in itself. I doubt you'll see any change out of three-quarters of a million euros, but I can get you some detailed costings. And I know a young couple who are very good project managers, they live fairly close by. That's if you want to go ahead."

"Toby, how about an algorithm on the probability?" Mark wondered.

"I'd rather take a bet on the outsider in the three-thirty at Chepstow," came the reply, and everyone laughed and relaxed.

***

During the next two months there were more meetings in London and on site; figures were produced, discussed and amended; legal and engineering reviews were carried out; and they met the mayor of the local commune of Saint Audan. Fortunately, though perhaps unsurprisingly, there did not appear to be any other potential buyers.

As time progressed they learned more about the history of the château. The original part was built in the fourteenth century for a farming family and comprised only the middle section of the existing structure. Clive had spotted the outlines of an old fireplace and chimney as well as a long-disappeared staircase and deduced that animals were kept here at ground level during the winter months while the family lived in the upper floor warmth and presumably got used to the odours. It was not until the early seventeenth century that the existing château was created.

Toby was not only brilliant at maths but also an avid researcher who knew his way around the library at the British Museum and how to ask the right questions. He tracked down Dr Alain Frugier, a professor in French history, and arranged to meet him one morning at a nearby coffee shop.

"Ah, medieval France, a time of great change," the professor enthused. "You have to remember that France, like much of Europe, was divided by religion from the early fifteen hundreds. First Martin Luther posted his theses in front of the castle church at Wittenburg and then John Calvin organised the first French – what we would now call Protestant – church in Strasbourg. To start with of course, those who renounced their Catholic faith were few. But the Inquisition with its bloody tactics of suppression did, may I say, a great job in convincing others of the merits of Protestantism, and by the end of the sixteenth century the new Calvinist beliefs and practices had spread throughout many parts of France, in particular the south-west."

He paused and Toby spoke.

"From what I've discovered and our architect has deduced we think the original building was converted into the château around sixteen hundred by a Huguenot family. Does that sound about right?"

"That could be," Dr Frugier said. "The reign of anti-Calvinist terror culminated on the twenty-fourth of August, 1572, with the Saint Bartholomew's Day massacre. At least five thousand killed in Toulouse alone. But this could not go on. King Henri the Fourth, who had himself grown up as a Calvinist, signed the Edict of Nantes in 1598 and for nearly one hundred years France, how would you say, drew a breath of relief. For the Calvinists in the south-west, many of whom were successful families engaged in the wool and leather trades, this was a time not to hide their wealth but to enjoy it in relative peace. It has always interested me that the original Huguenots, as they came to be called, were mostly middle and upper-class families who left the Catholic church to avoid paying its huge taxes, as much as anything, while the poor and the peasantry had nothing much material to lose but were offered an afterlife by their priests."

Toby swung the conversation away from religion.

"Yes, interesting. Now after it was rebuilt, we believe that the château housed at least three generations of the de Malecare family who were very important lawyers in Toulouse through to the eighteenth century. It's interesting to speculate whether another lawyer, better known to future generations as a groundbreaking mathematician, Pierre de Fermat, would ever have visited the house, as he was active at this time in Castres, not too far away, where he was buried."

"Ah, Pierre de Fermat!" Dr Frugier exclaimed. "We must be one of the few countries in the world who do not honour an international, dare I say it, genius. You see, very few of us actually understand what he was trying to prove. Mathematics is not a national strong point. But I digress. Whoever owned the château through the late eighteenth century and the Revolution would probably have had a hard time because the local population, particularly the gentry, changed sides quite frequently. And remember that many documents relating to these old buildings were lost or destroyed."

Toby nodded in agreement.

"Yes," he said. "Our *notaire* tells us that it wasn't until well into Napoleon Bonaparte's reign in the early eighteen hundreds that there were records showing a new family as the owners. My researches indicate that this family, the de Montforts, were also lawyers and became involved in politics. One of them, Jean, was elected to the national parliament in 1871 at the end of the Franco-Prussian War and began a political dynasty which survived into the twenty-first century."

"Ah yes," Dr Frugier mused. "Now you have mentioned a family that became pretty well known. If my memory serves me correctly, by 1914 the family de Montfort was well entrenched both in parliament and senior roles in the finance ministry. Then young Xavier de Montfort consolidated their fame and fortune by earning a Croix de Guerre fighting alongside Marshall Pétain at Verdun, which was the decisive battle of the First World War. After leaving the army he stood successfully for a parliamentary seat representing Toulouse and also took control of the family firm, which was heavily involved in the huge business of wool processing based around Castres and Mazamet. That is where they lived and prospered, and they used your château as their country retreat.

"But Xavier's relationship with Pétain came close to being his downfall during the Second World War. When the Marshall created and led the Vichy Government in 1940 he offered Xavier the role of finance minister, which he accepted. He moved with his family first to Vichy and later to Paris, where he played an important part in liaising on financial matters with the occupying German forces. After the war he was tried on charges of collaboration, but escaped conviction on what some would regard as the spurious grounds that his contribution actually had some positive results for France, and also that he played no part in the deportations or executions of Jews and resistance fighters. Nevertheless his political career was finished and much of his property was confiscated, so he probably took refuge in your château."

"Well, thank you for your time and your learned insight, Dr Frugier," Toby said. "You've certainly given me a lot to think about. As we understand the current situation, it is the widow – and second wife – of Xavier who is the owner of the château and the neighbouring farm where she lives. It sounds as if things have not gone well for the family de Montfort over the last few years, because the château is almost derelict. It will be interesting to find out more."

"And I shall be happy to learn more of your venture into the history of France. Thank you for the coffee, Toby, and I hope to see you again soon."

2.

THE REALITY

GETTING to the stage of signing and exchanging contracts was a new experience for the whole family, and quite different from the process in England.

They were told that normal practice was for both parties to have the same *notaire*, but they were wary of this after also being advised to obtain the authorisations for alterations and new building work critical to acquiring the property before contracts were exchanged. Therefore, once the purchase price had been agreed on verbally, they appointed their own *notaire*, a Maitre Buffard, on the recommendation of a colleague of Mark and Pru's son, Christopher.

The two *notaires* drew up a *compromis de vente*, a provisional sales contract, and both parties were invited to meet at Buffard's office, review the document and, if in agreement, sign. It was then largely up to the vendor to obtain the necessary authorisations.

The meeting in Maitre Buffard's office was the first time Mark, Toby and Clive met Yvette de Montfort, the owner of the château, who in her late seventies was still quite a beautiful woman. They could see why Xavier had been attracted to her sixty years ago. She was accompanied by a man in a suit and tie who had "banker" written all over him, and she did not look happy. The *notaire* for Yvette – who also acted for her mortgage-owning bank – went through the documentation clause by clause and Maitre Buffard translated when necessary. The purchase price and the codicils relating to planning authorisations were all agreed to without difficulty. It was only when they came to a clause requiring the vendor to remove some asbestos found in the building survey that Madame de Montfort broke her silence.

"Why at my cost?" she demanded.

Her banker put out a restraining hand.

"It is absolutely normal," he said.

Madame de Montfort slapped her papers on Buffard's desk.

"It is always I who have to pay," she snapped back, and didn't say another word, not even *au revoir* when the meeting broke up.

***

Planning permission to convert the old mill into a self-contained apartment with access to the château involved tedious on-site meetings with a platoon of bureaucrats, who had to submit their findings and recommendations for dealing with arcane issues like the effect on local agriculture, and whether the increase in living space conformed with strict guidelines. Furthermore, the swimming pool approval was infuriatingly complicated by the paperwork needed to install the housing for the water pump and the motor to operate the heavy-duty pool cover.

Although the mayor of Saint Audan seemed willing to assist in this drawn-out process, letters had to be written to various government departments and plans submitted. It all took several months and repeated visits by Mark and Clive, but eventually the go-ahead was given. As Clive liked to say, "Hey, welcome to France, the world capital of bureaucracy." Once the authorisations were approved contracts were exchanged, and two months later the château changed ownership.

For the renovation work, Clive recommended retaining a local British manager who was bilingual and had already costed the project and assembled a team of artisans, rather than employing a builder with sub-contractors who would be out to make a profit on everything. The manager, Garth, assured them that he had used his artisans before, and so, eight months after falling in love with the château at first sight, they were up and away.

Visits to the château were made regularly during the twelve months of renovations and sometimes, particularly when she was covered in scaffolding and appeared to be blindfolded, the old lady looked very old indeed and very unhappy. But as cars carrying the two British families, her new owners, turned into the driveway the day the job was finished, she seemed to be almost smiling, like a younger woman in fresh clothes, showing off her brand new windows and the newly painted shutters agleam in the sunlight.

Mark had organised domestic helpers to make everything shipshape and greet the new occupants.

"May I introduce you to my wife, Madame Escott, and to her sister, Madame Burlington, who is the wife of Monsieur Burlington," he said to the small welcoming party, who smiled back pleasantly. "This is Alice," he said to his wife and sister-in-law. "Alice has agreed to work for us on a regular basis with general housekeeping duties and see that everything is kept in good order when we are not here."

Then Mark introduced Bernard, the head gardener, and his

assistant, François. Everyone shook hands and Alice led the ladies into the house while the gardeners helped Mark and Toby unload the cars.

After a lot of discussion it had been agreed that Toby and his family would take the *gite* in the mill and Mark and his family would have the larger west wing of the château, since Mark was nearer to retirement and would be spending more time in France.

This visit, their first as an extended family, was in mid-April, early spring, coinciding with Easter. Tulips were in abundance, the lilac bushes along the driveway were flowering and rose beds were being planted. Mark and Bernard had worked out how to make four rose bushes climb the south-facing front wall of the château, and soon it would be adorned by a magnificent display of colour.

Mark and Pru had brought along with them their son Chris, his wife Diane, and their two children, Chloe and Joey, who were five and three. Toby and Jenny had their two daughters, Sarah, who was five months pregnant and whose husband would be joining them for the weekend, and her younger sister Lucy.

It was quite a house-full, and Pru and Jenny had spent the flight from London working out a schedule of domestic duties, including a kitchen roster and menu suggestions. A visit to the supermarket was arranged for later that afternoon and the shopping list was formidable, despite Alice already stocking up on staples such as bread, milk and eggs.

The girls, all five of them, were excited at the prospect of their first shopping spree in France and set off for the local branch of E. Leclerc, which lay in a commercial zone just outside the nearest town. Lucy took the children – and a dictionary – to look for some of the more exotic items on the list like Skippy peanut butter, a favourite of Toby's, and horse radish sauce to go with the roast beef, while Pru and Jenny bought a few bottles of wine.

They filled their order, obtained a Leclerc loyalty card, and took two trolley loads to a friendly checkout cashier. A few minutes later and several hundred euros lighter they were on the way home, mission accomplished.

In E. Leclerc they saw an advertisement for an Easter egg hunt over the long weekend in a local park, which sounded like fun for the little ones, so they decided to try it out on Good Friday.

It was not quite what they expected, but Chloe and Joey seemed keen to join in the hourly egg hunts which adults were overseeing in a fenced-off field. To start the fun, older children were given baskets containing different coloured eggs and instructions to hide each one in a different part of the field.

Then the little ones set off to find six eggs, one of each colour. Encouraged by shouts, suggestions and cries of despair from their parents, they'd run around, sometimes forgetting about the eggs and crying because they couldn't see mum or dad. Then the older kids were allowed to go and help their siblings. Chloe raced in to support her little brother and they came back clutching their baskets with the right-coloured eggs. After the eggs were counted, the children were given tickets which they took to a van and exchanged for a real chocolate Easter egg.

For the new owners of the château it was an interesting first lesson in the culture of this complicated European nation: in France, no one person may carry out a task which two could do equally well.

The Easter weekend also seemed like a good opportunity to meet other members of the commune. Mark had already met the mayor at the *Mairie* on several occasions while negotiating the property purchase, and he had proven to be friendly and generally helpful. Thus the mayor and his wife agreed to visit the château for an *apero* on Easter Saturday evening.

Michel Ricard was a man well into his sixties with iron-grey hair and a voice with all the inflections and accents that indicated he was a local boy. This he confirmed on arrival.

"I was born here of a farming family and I've lived here all my life," the mayor said with pride. "Two generations ago we were tenant farmers working for the Vicomte de LaPrade, but two wars and many changes in agricultural practices have given us the opportunity of acquiring the land, about ninety hectares, which we now farm for our own benefit. My wife Adilah was born in Morocco. We have a son and a daughter, but neither of them want a life in farming – they have seen how hard it is. Still, we have hopes that one of our grandsons, should we have one, will take it on. We shall see."

His wife was a stunning and much younger woman, tall and slim with the black hair and tanned skin that distinguished so many from North Africa.

"We welcome you to Saint Audan," Adilah said. "It is good to have the château restored and occupied." She turned to Pru and Jenny. "You must feel free to ask me for any help or information which may be of benefit to you. My husband is certainly the mayor, but sometimes we women know best the ways to achieve the result we desire."

"Quite so," said Pru with a knowing smile.

Most of the English group were struggling with the language: although they all spoke a smattering of French, the local accent with words like *maintenant* coming out like *mainten-ung* and a tendency to slide one word into the next made it hard going. Mark was leading for the home team.

"Well, it is really good to see you again and meet Madame Ricard at last, and thank you for coming, Michel," he said.

Michel accepted a *pastis* and water ("but no ice please") while Adilah asked for a *blanc doux*, which fortunately had been on the girls' shopping list.

When they were all seated, with a drink in hand, Mark had a question. "You would have seen many changes in the commune, including this building. Can you tell us a bit about it?"

"This house has been the centre of much unhappiness and discord for many years," said Michel. "When Xavier de Montfort came to live here in disgrace in 1948 he brought with him his wife, Elene, and their two daughters. You know, I think, that he had been accused of collaborating with the Nazis, and he was lucky not to be shot by the partisans when they took control of Paris briefly in 1944." Mark and the others nodded. "But his business was compulsorily acquired from him under a law of the de Gaulle government and he was left with the château and the farm – and quite a bit of cash, as well as a property in Paris which he kept quiet about. But things got worse. Elene became very sick and Xavier had to hire a nurse to care for her. He knew nothing about farming and was frequently *arnaqué*. You understand that?"

"Scammed or cheated," Mark translated.

"Yes, *arnaqué* by his suppliers, his workers, and those to whom he sold his produce. And then in 1954 Elene died. She was just forty-six and her two daughters had grown up, married and moved to Paris. I was not old enough to remember the funeral, which was a very quiet affair. Her body is interred in the family vault in the cemetery of the church here in Saint Audan."

Michel accepted a refill and continued.

"Xavier appeared to be heartbroken, but less than a year later he married Elene's nurse, Yvette."

"What was the attitude of the commune to that marriage?" asked Toby, making an attempt at French.

"It is interesting that you ask," replied Michel. "The commune had always been divided over Xavier. For some he was the descendant of a long line, almost like aristocrats, and for others he was just another damned Parisian . . . and you know we hate them even more than we hate *les étrangers*, you foreigners!" He had the grace to say that with a smile. "Yvette was nearly forty years younger than Xavier and only just of an age to be legally married. Xavier avoided an outcry by having a very private civil ceremony and no public celebrations. So it seemed he might rekindle a happy life, especially when two sons were born soon afterwards. But he had again sown the seeds of discord."

Michel sipped his *pastis* and paused.

"You wish that I continue?" he asked, and everyone nodded.

"According to documents on the public record, Xavier gave significant sums of money, which he raised by selling what remained of his business assets, to the two daughters from his first marriage. In return, they renounced the rights to their inheritance. In what was said to be his last will and testament, he then bequeathed the château and its land and the farm buildings to one son, Jean-Paul, and the property in Paris to Christian, his brother. But stories later circulated that the will was not in his hand, and possibly not even the signature. His sons were of very different temperaments and interests. After attending agricultural college, Jean-Paul went back to the château and managed the estate. He never married and he lived there with his mother. Christian, on the other hand, managed to gain admission to Sciences Po, the Paris Institute of Political Studies, and then the *École National d'Administration*, where politicians of all persuasions and most senior bureaucrats go. It was the 'open sesame' to a career in his father's footsteps and he gained a junior position in the ministry of finance. Then Xavier died. He was an old man and very tired. He had lived through two World Wars and probably still thought he had done his best for France in both, but he had been accused of treason and lived half his life in the shadow of disgrace."

"Did his sons get on?" Toby asked.

"When the will was produced Christian was furious," Michel replied. "He said not only was the division of the estate totally unbalanced – which under French inheritance law could certainly be challenged – he had always understood that he and his brother would become the joint owners of the château. Jean-Paul would not cede his inheritance and he was supported by their mother who, in any case, had the usual life tenancy of the matrimonial home. It was a war of words to start with that became a legal battle. Jean-Paul had little money and only the income from the farm and some tenancies to support himself and his mother and maintain the château, so he was soon borrowing money to pay his legal fees and taking out mortgages on the estate. He appealed to his brother, but Christian was implacable: either hand the château over to him or be ruined, which he eventually was. Jean-Paul's lawyers recommended the legal separation of the château and the farming estate, and he did that, but both were soon heavily encumbered. In the end Christian won. He got a ruling in his favour, but the château and the farm virtually belonged to the banks so there was nothing for him to take back. And although he was reasonably well off, he did not have enough money to pay out the loans and settle with his brother, who had by now contracted lung cancer. It claimed him almost twenty years after their father died."

Michel then explained that Jean-Paul and Yvette had moved into the farmhouse, and she continued to support herself after he died by renting out a *gite* and some *chambres d'hote* for lodgers in the château to curb the maintenance costs. But it mostly lay empty and uncared for, the debts were mounting, and after Jean-

Paul died Yvette could not even pay the interest on the mortgages, which now far exceeded the value of the two properties. But the banks were not keen to press for a sale as they would have to absorb their losses.

"So that is almost the end of the long story," Michel said with a sigh. "You have bought and restored the château, Yvette still lives in the farmhouse, and Christian is a *deputé* with a portfolio in the government of President Hollande."

Mark spoke for all of them.

"Thank you so much, Michel. It has been a fascinating trip through your local history, and you have enlightened us about the château and its past. We very much hope that we can contribute to the life and well-being of the commune."

"You will I'm sure," the mayor replied, "and I would recommend that the first thing to do is become acquainted with your fellow *communards*. Why not come next month to the lunch held on the Sunday of the village fete?"

Mark raised his glass to that suggestion and shortly afterwards the party broke up.

3.

GETTING TO KNOW YOU

MOST members of the two families decided to return for the village fete, and in the meantime Mark and Pru stayed on to enjoy the château in tranquillity.

They made themselves known to their neighbours and met Yvette de Montfort again, who was much more at ease than on their initial encounter. She invited them into her farmhouse but was reluctant to accept an invitation to visit the château where her children were born and she had spent so many years. However, a few days later she rang the doorbell and asked if it was convenient to come in and have a look.

Pru showed her every room, taking nearly an hour as she explained the full extent of the renovations. Yvette didn't utter a word until they were sitting in the main salon, where she accepted a glass of wine and wept.

"It is wonderful to see the old house again," she said, regaining her composure. "And you have made it so beautiful and so different too. I hardly remember how it used to be."

"We are so pleased that you came and we understand how hard it must be for you," Pru said. "But we want you to know that you are welcome at any time, and when you feel like it we would love to hear about your life here. You must have some wonderful memories."

Yvette handed back her almost untouched drink.

"And some not so wonderful, Pru. Yes, I will do that, but it is too emotional for me now. Perhaps I could come back another time and then I will tell you what life at Château du Moulin was like in the nineteen fifties."

A date was agreed upon and Yvette left.

***

The mayor was hospitable and eager to introduce the new residents to people who might be interesting or useful to them. One was a doctor, Antoine Lefevre, a handsome and amiable man in his late forties who had been raised in Toulouse before taking over a practice in Castres twenty years ago.

"And are you still happy in Castres?" Pru asked him.

"Yes," he said. "Castres is a relatively small town, about forty-four thousand inhabitants, and you can easily become involved in lots of activities – the sport, the politics and, I must say, as a bachelor I am frequently invited to dinner parties to, how do you say it, make up the numbers. Michel tells me you are a pianist, Madame, and I have the privilege of belonging to a group of amateur musicians who enjoy giving small concerts and recitals. I myself play the *violoncello*, the cello I think in English, and Madame Ricard often joins us, Adilah. She has a beautiful voice."

"Is that so? We met her recently with her husband, the mayor. That sounds like an excellent idea, Doctor Lefevre. We have a piano at the château in a room where we could give small concerts. We will invite you to play for us very soon."

"And I would be delighted to accept. Tell me, are you planning to spend much time here? Because if you are, you should think about getting your healthcare issues in order. I believe our services are some of the best, but as with so many things in France there is always a lot of paperwork. And sometimes just finding a doctor prepared to take on new patients can be difficult. I have no wish to push myself, but I should be happy to see you at my *cabinet,* my surgery, if that would be of help to you."

Pru was happy to accept his offer and they set a rendezvous for the following week.

Mark and Pru also met the Ricards' children. Louisa was in her early twenties and had the same strong build as her father, combined with the dark good looks and vivacity of her mother. She had a master's degree in marketing and was working for a major fashion label in Toulouse. Laurent was a precociously intelligent boy of sixteen studying to take his *baccalaureat*. He was a slighter build than his sister but also dark-haired, and while gracious and friendly he lacked her exuberance. He told Mark and Pru he was concentrating on the sciences, but had not yet made up his mind about a career.

"I have done some holiday work in a pharmacy," Laurent said, "and I find the huge advances in medical knowledge which are happening ever more frequently are really fascinating. But I must also recognise that the medical profession faces a future where more and more diagnosis will be carried out by what you call, I think, artificial intelligence. The next decades will be revolutionary."

He smiled, and Pru, who was hugely impressed by his intellect, told him about her work at the music therapy centre and invited him to visit if he was ever in London. Laurent agreed that in France the treatment of people, particularly children, with neurological or psychological problems was woefully behind much of the western world.

"Perhaps I should consider becoming a psychoanalyst," he mused. "I don't know exactly where I wish to be in ten years' time."

Pru and Mark invited Louisa and Laurent to come to the château to socialise during the summer holidays and they readily agreed.

At another *apero* to which they were invited by the mayor and his wife they met Lionel Cros, a neighbouring farmer who was one of the two *adjoints*, deputy mayors. Cros was a name that cropped up frequently in this region, and Lionel came from a family of four brothers and two sisters aged from their late sixties to their early eighties who were all born in the commune. The brothers were still living there but the sisters had married and moved away. Their father, like the mayor's, had been a tenant farmer, and the boys grew up being expected to carry on the family tradition. But the post-war environment and a better education gave two of them different ideas and ambitions: one became a builder and one an electrician, while Lionel and the other brother stayed on the land. They made a good pair, as the eldest boy had a head for commerce and improved the family's finances by concentrating their farming activities in the areas of greatest return, leaving Lionel to the day-to-day property management.

Lionel Cros told Mark about some of the ways the family had built up its fortunes.

"To start with, we owned very little land ourselves, but after the war many of the big landowners were short of cash, and when inheritance and wealth taxes were brought in by the government they had to sell at a very low price. We borrowed money and bought up. The old landowners were seen driving towards Switzerland in their Mercedes, carrying big suitcases full of French francs. Back then, up to the nineteen fifties, every farmer's aim was to be self-supporting, so we kept a few cows, a few pigs and chickens, as well as growing our own vegetables alongside the crops for selling. Not good. So the cows and pigs went, and we concentrated on growing the most profitable crops and left our wives to look after the hens and a few vegetables." He smiled. "And that's why my generation has had fewer babies!"

Lionel then outlined an interesting scheme the government came up with in the nineteen fifties.

"If the whole commune agreed, a valuer would look at everyone's bundle of small fields, which had been accumulated but also divided between family members. Then we could swap individual lots, so that each family got a parcel of land that was consolidated into a smaller number of bigger fields. This was very important because tractors were replacing our ploughs and fewer farmhands were needed. Having two brothers who were artisans was useful too. As we acquired land we gained certain rights to build houses for ourselves, which we did."

"It sounds like you have done very well, Lionel," Mark said. "If I ever want to take up farming I know who to turn to."

This *apero dinatoire* turned out to be a long evening with a variety of dishes, some small like Spanish tapas, accompanied by different wines greatly enjoyed by the other guests, who regaled themselves while continuing to talk loudly. The English couple soon discovered that most of the local men over fifty were very deaf, almost certainly from spending three or more decades on a noisy tractor without ear protection. Mark and Pru found the whole event tiring but did their best to join in a few conversations, which seemed to revolve around how the weather was not helping this year's crop of wheat, maize, sunflowers and soya. They came to realise that this was the principal and sometimes only topic when French farmers got together.

The other deputy mayor was also present, Julien Deschamps, an electrician, and both deputies were accompanied by their wives, who Pru tried to engage about life in the commune, with little success. After staying for three hours she and Mark thanked the mayor and his wife for making them so welcome, promised to be at the fete next week, and took their leave.

***

One morning, as arranged, Yvette de Montfort knocked on the front door and Pru and Mark welcomed her in for her second visit to the château. This time she was keen to talk.

"If you permit I will try to tell you my story in English," she said. "I was used to doing that with my sons, but since a long time I have had little practice. So I begin many, many years ago, when I was just a young girl who had a small experience in nursing. My parents had so many children it was not *supportable* – bearable? – to live at home, so I needed a job and a roof. And I found them with Xavier . . . and Elene of course. She was not yet fifty but had already undergone surgery for breast cancer, and this was in the days when chemotherapy and radiotherapy were just being discovered. She was dying.

"It was very painful for her, and perhaps even more so in a way for Xavier. He still felt he had been badly treated after the war. Yes he collaborated with the Germans, but he kept food and other essentials coming into Paris and the other big cities, and he was not found to be complicit in rounding up Jews or other atrocities. When he was released from prison after he was found not guilty of war crimes he just hoped for some years of happiness with Elene and their daughters back at the château. But there was Elene's illness, and also in the countryside for several years after the war a lot of people declared that they were always *résistants*. Many of them would have nothing to do with Xavier or his family. Believe me, some of those old and terrible fractures within families and between neighbours are not yet healed . . . even after three generations."

Mark and Pru glanced at each other as she dabbed a tear with a tissue.

"So . . . when Elene died, their daughters had left home and I still needed that roof over my head. I comforted Xavier as best I could. He was very respectful and never took advantage of me, but the commune did not know that. Here was a man old enough to be my grandfather living with an eighteen year-old woman, disgusting. So he asked me to marry him and I agreed. And of course we made love. He was very gentle and I liked it. For the first time in my life I had love, security and warmth. Then Jean-Paul and Christian were born and Xavier and I were very happy, but sadly, only for a few years."

Yvette explained how Jean-Paul was a kind and gentle child who doted on his little brother, but Christian became demanding and aggressive, taking Jean-Paul's toys and frequently trying to hurt him. She likened it to the story of Cain and Abel in the bible. The boys were sent to separate schools to give Jean-Paul a chance of finding his own friends, and they went on to follow very different career paths.

"Christian moved to Paris in his early twenties and is married, but without children. I hardly ever see him or his wife. Jean-Paul stayed at home until his father died and then, I think you say, all hell let loose. When the will was produced, *bon Dieu!* Christian was incandescent when he was left out of the joint ownership of the château and its property. As you would know, French inheritance law normally demands that all the assets of the deceased are divided equally amongst the children, and often this proves very difficult if one wants to retain a house and the other does not. But for us this was not the case – both boys wanted the château."

"We can understand that," Pru remarked.

"Jean-Paul would not give in," Yvette said, shaking her fist. "Perhaps he wanted revenge for all those years of bullying. So Christian started hiring smart Paris lawyers and we had to do the same. There is a *tribunal* for every dispute in France, and these things take years and lots of money. Fifteen years later Jean-Paul could fight no longer – no money left, the château falling into disrepair, and the two of us forced to move into the farmhouse. Another heart broken, another family ruined. In the end Christian won, but it was, I believe, a Pyrrhic victory, *n'est-ce pas?* The château and the farm had mortgages much higher than their sale value, and I had the right of a lifetime tenancy even after Jean-Paul died. The banks got some of their money back when you bought the château, and now they are pressuring me to put the farm on the market for nearly a million euros, which is what is owed. But it's not worth much more than half of that. And I am still here, which is about the end of my sad story."

Mark and Pru looked at each other for a long moment and then Pru spoke up.

"We are deeply saddened too by your story. Families can be strange things. We are blessed so far with one that enjoys things together and has few disagreements. Thank you for telling us all that, Yvette, and if we can ever be of any help please do not hesitate to contact us."

***

A month later it was much warmer, the days were longer, and Bernard's cherished roses were in full bloom. The pergola was erected on the outside dining area and a long table and a dozen comfortable chairs were in readiness for the next invasion of visitors.

While thinking about invasions, Pru came across an article in *La Dépêche*, the regional daily newspaper, which threw an interesting light on the attitudes of some of the local inhabitants.

A petition against an invasion of midges

Within a radius of about one kilometre between Lautrec and Jonquières, a dozen inhabitants have recently signed a petition in respect to an invasion of midges in their houses. These habitations are in the neighbourhood of a farmer of Jonquières, Fabien L., a producer and supplier of onions. But Monsieur L. does not take his unsold onions to the garbage tip and merely puts them onto the border of his property, which is also the edge of a watercourse and the *voie verte* from Castres to Albi. The odour they give off cannot leave anyone indifferent. This odour and the midges which come with it have provoked the exasperation of Isabelle R. who carries on a business of *gites* and *chambres d'hote* at her property about 200 metres from the aforesaid L. but exactly in the path of the Autan when it blows.

"I am the most affected, I put up with the smell of rotting onions and now with the arrival of warm weather it's the midge invasion," says Isabelle, who launched the petition. She shows us two jars containing hundreds of midges: "I've just had some German tourists, they put vinegar and sugar in these pots and here is what they collected."

Isabelle's property is in the community of Lautrec and she therefore contacted the mayor, T.B., "who can do nothing because L's property is in the commune of Jonquières." So she contacted the mayor of Jonquières, J-P L. "He has not reacted to our demands so I'm going over his head to get a time limit on these insanitary nuisances which have been poisoning our lives for several years."

"Since they've been here these people have done nothing but annoy us," replies the mother of L., who wasn't available yesterday for business reasons. She explains however that the garbage in question is being cleared. "It's just temporary because we couldn't get rid of it because of the weather: it was impractical," says Madame L. who adds that this neighbour "about 800 metres away" makes one petition after another against them. "Last time it was because of the noise of the fans which dry the onions for us," she affirms, while letting us hear that her neighbour wants the advantages of the country without the inconveniences.

Maybe something to bear in mind, Pru thought.

4.

A BIG WEEKEND

IT WAS the weekend of the annual fete, and although the inhabitants of the commune numbered only five hundred the committee had organised several events, some to attract visitors from neighbouring villages. On the Saturday evening there would be a rock band and dancing, the *Repas Campagnard* was the Sunday lunch and, because it happened to be one of the many national holidays in May, a *vide grenier,* which was like a car-boot sale, had been organised for the Monday.

The English contingent at the château was ready for all of it, but they decided to divide their forces. Chris and Diane were leaving their children with the grandparents and going to the Saturday evening festivities with Sarah and Lucy, while on the Sunday, Mark and Pru, Toby and Jenny and the two girls would attend the lunch.

Like many evening events in southern France, the band took to the stage quite late, at ten o'clock, but was soon into some Johnny Hallyday numbers and had the crowd on their feet. Sarah, almost six months pregnant, took it slowly and carefully with her husband Tom, who was enjoying his first visit to the château. Lucy, however, was overwhelmed by boys and young men wanting to dance with her, and she didn't refuse.

The night was warm and clear and those not dancing, or just taking a break, could sit under the clear moon and enjoy drinks and hamburgers cooked on a big open barbecue. Everyone under sixty from the commune was there and some of the elderly as well.

Chris had been coming to France with his parents and sisters for as long as he could remember and he loved the entertainment, as did Diane. By midnight, however, they agreed with Sarah and Tom that it was time to head home. But where was Lucy?

Tom scanned the dance floor, couldn't see her, and walked around the marquee. There she was, in the arms of a good-looking young Frenchman. Tom coughed politely and Lucy relinquished her grip . . . slightly.

"Can we help you, sir?" she asked cheekily.

"We thought . . . well, we think we need to be getting Sarah home," her brother-in-law said, "and we only have one car."

Lucy turned back to her new friend and said, "Yves, do you have a car? And could you give me a lift back to the château a bit later on?"

"But of course, Lucy, and I would love to have another dance with you," he said in good English with a strong accent. "And I promise to bring her back by, say, trois heures, M'sieur."

Sarah was a bit apprehensive when Tom reported back, but not Diane. "I know your sister pretty well, Sarah, and she's had three years away at university. I think she can look after herself."

So the four of them left and Lucy enjoyed a few more hours in the arms of her new beau.

Next morning they were congregated in the big kitchen, with Pru and Jenny cooking scrambled eggs as Chris made the coffee. The early morning sun was streaming in and it promised to be a perfect day. They moved out to the terrace where Chloe and Joey could play, and just before ten Lucy appeared to a round of applause.

"Darling, well done," Toby, her father, said with a smile. "We understand you have captured the hearts of every male inhabitant of our commune under the age of thirty in just one evening."

Lucy was too tired to blush.

"His name is Yves," she said. "And he is helping to serve the lunch at the fete, so you will all get to meet him."

***

The lunch was billed as starting at twelve-thirty. The family were there on time, and several dozen people were already in or outside the big marquee where drinks were being served: *pastis*, a sweet white wine or beer. Mark had advised the organisers that he was booking for seven, and as he walked up to the table where the money was being collected he wondered what they would be getting for the fifteen-euro ticket price. He went into the dining hall to reserve seven places and saw the mayor, who asked if they would like to sit next to him and his family. Mark gratefully accepted.

More people arrived, many of whom Mark and Pru now knew, and the rest of the family were greeted warmly with kisses from the women – left cheek first, then the right – and strong handshakes from the men. The children in attendance followed their parents' example, politely greeting these strange people from, they were told, another country.

The drinking went on until one-thirty, by which time the English were tiring of trying to cope with the language. None of the other guests appeared to speak a word of English. "And why should they?" said Pru."You wouldn't find too many people in the middle of Somerset who speak French."

When everyone was seated, a well-dressed man walked in and headed straight for the mayor, who sprang to his feet and embraced him.

"*Mesdames et Messieurs*," the mayor called out, "if I could have your attention. Most of you know Christian de Montfort, our *deputé*, who has been kind enough to give up some of his time to come to our gathering today to greet you and say a few words. Christian . . ."

There was a round of appreciative applause.

"Thank you, *Monsieur le Maire*," Christian said, and spoke in the confident tone of a politician used to working a crowd. "It is always a great pleasure to come to Saint Audan and congratulate your mayor, the *conseil*, and particularly the committee on putting on such a good fete. My friends, in these troubled times it is more important than ever that we remain together, loyal to our principles and the great traditions of France. In this so peaceful part of our country you may feel far removed from the events which are shaking the world, but your voices must be heard by those who make the decisions, because those decisions will affect the lives of your children and grandchildren. Be strong, my friends, and put back into power those who have your best interests at heart. Thank you, and *Vive la République!*"

Nearly everyone in the room stood and applauded as Christian de Montfort walked down each row of chairs, touching every extended hand. His expression did not change: his mouth smiled but not the dark eyes. He reminded Mark of a deadly brown snake he had seen in the bush on a trip to Australia. In less than five minutes the *deputé* was gone.

When they were all reseated the mayor rose to his feet again.

"And now I would like to introduce you to some new arrivals

in our little commune. They come from England," he said, holding up his hand, "but at least they are not from Paris." Laughter, cheering and clapping broke out. "You will know already that they have bought and renovated the old château, and it has become *magnifique* again after so many years. *Bon!* They are Madame et Monsieur Escott, Madame et Monsieur Burlington, and their daughters and, so far, one young husband." They stood up as he called out their names and their fellow guests got to their feet as the room applauded. "We wish them well here in our little commune."

The family inclined their heads, said *"Merci"* to the mayor, and were relieved that a reply *en Français* was not called for.

Then the food arrived in the hands of the younger members of the committee: big platters of *charcuterie*, salad and a selection of dressing, baskets of bread, plus bottles of white and red wine and jugs of water. People had been asked to bring their own *couverts* – plates, cutlery and glasses – and they dived in hungrily.

Conversation resumed after the initial self-serving was finished and Toby found himself in an exchange with another neighbour, a young farmer who had set himself up to produce vegetables and fruit which he sold at his small holding as well as the local markets. His name was Daniel and he spoke good English.

"I have been very lucky," Daniel said. "I had the chance to go to Australia for a year when I left school, before agricultural college. I had a great time and travelled very much. I mostly earned money by working on the land – and the land there is so big! – picking fruit and so on. They use a lot of machinery too, so I sought out the vegetable growers and learned their methods, which has helped me very much. Please come and visit me, I am open on Tuesday evenings. The other days I go to bed early as I have to get to the markets by six in the morning to secure the place for my stand."

Yves appeared from the kitchen, walked over to Lucy, bent down and kissed her on both cheeks. Then he straightened up and Lucy introduced him to her father, mother, sister, brother-in-law, aunt and uncle. Yves shook their hands, with a *"Bonjour"* to each one, and stood behind Lucy's chair. He said he was delighted to meet them all and hoped to talk later, but now he must return to the kitchen. Squeezing Lucy's shoulder, he left.

The main course was *cuisse de canard*, duck legs served on a bed of lentils and vegetables in a delicious sauce heavy with garlic and thyme. Everybody helped themselves and the wine flowed freely. The young members of the committee patrolled the aisles between the four long dining tables replenishing the bread and wine.

"I don't know how they do all this for fifteen euros a head," said Jenny. "The food alone would cost that in a restaurant, without all the wine we're getting through."

Lucy told them almost all of the food was grown by members of the commune.

"You remember that huge duck farm towards Saint Patrick?" she said. "They sell all this to the committee at a very good price and people like Daniel, who's sitting next to Dad, provide the vegetables. Yves is studying to be a chef and he was telling me this last night."

Tom interjected. "I'm surprised you had time to discuss the local economy, Lucy."

"You would be surprised at the things we discussed, Tom. The local economy, family relationships . . . all sorts of things," she said suggestively.

It was nearly three o'clock when the tables were cleared and dessert came out: plates of cheese followed by ice cream on a stick.

"Well the first two courses were terrific, so I guess we can't complain about the finale," Jenny declared. "I'll definitely come again."

For the last half hour a DJ had been playing reasonably soft music, but now he put on a loud number which was evidently a well-known local piece. Everyone waved their serviettes to and fro over their heads in time with the rhythm and some sang. Then a dozen male members of the committee appeared from the kitchen, dressed as nuns or monks of the Carmelite Order. Jumping up on the stage, they started to dance as provocatively as decency would allow, revealing a lot of men's underpants.

"Wow," Toby gaped. "You wouldn't get this at a Rotary lunch in Surrey."

As the music pounded, the "Carmelites" jumped off the stage, pulled diners from their chairs, and led them to the dance floor. One of the nuns was Yves, who looked quite cute in a brown habit. He picked Lucy as "sister's" partner while a bearded nun curtsied in front of Tom and offered his hand. People stood and applauded, and other committee members began to roll up the paper covering the tables, which they stacked against the walls. Then all the locals joined in the dancing.

Mark looked questioningly at the rest of the family.

"Time to go with the flow," said Jenny, and as they went forward together they were split up and passed around. It seemed like everyone wanted to dance with the new clan in the château.

After thirty minutes of fun everyone was flagging, especially Sarah. They sat down beside the mayor and his wife, and thanked him for making them feel at home.

"As I said, we are very happy to have you in our commune," Monsieur Ricard replied. "And please feel free to come and see

43

me if you have any problems. Once this weekend is over Adilah and I will have more time to spend with you, and we shall hope to see you at our home."

They said their goodbyes and returned to the château – six of them. Lucy was missing again.

"Well, just the *vide grenier* to go tomorrow," Mark announced as he uncorked a bottle of red and slumped in a comfy chair after all that exertion. "And then, if we're still up for it, a sightseeing trip to Albi on Tuesday, clear up and clean up on Wednesday, and off home on Thursday. That will give us a full weekend to gird our loins for whatever awaits us next week. And I need to earn some money."

So the next day they set off again for the *Mairie* and the *salle de fetes* where the *vide grenier* was taking place. For such a small community there seemed to be a lot of stallholders, but at least twenty were manned by "professionals" from outside the community. The locals' stands mostly offered secondhand clothes for children, as well as toys that had been outgrown, no-longer-wanted crockery, and garden tools that needed a bit of loving care. Nothing took their fancy, but it was interesting to recognise the new-found faces and have a chat, and by noon they were in the beer tent which was doing good business on a very hot day.

An hour later they were back at the château enjoying the cold lunch Pru and Jenny had prepared in advance, with some of the chilled *rosé* from Gaillac they had all come to like.

On their first visit to Albi they drove for an hour through beautiful countryside and gently rolling hills stocked with grazing cattle. The steeper slopes were still heavily wooded, and everywhere was green.

They were in three cars and Lucy was extremely happy because Yves had managed to get the day off to accompany them. This was useful, as he knew the city well. On his advice they stopped in a big open car park and set off for the cathedral.

Yves explained that the Cathedral of Sainte Cécile was quite unique. It was thought to be the biggest brick building in the world and had a massive belltower over seventy-five metres in height. The main entrance was through a door on its southern flank.

"The cathedral started out as a fortress following the dreadful slaughter of the crusade against the Cathars," Yves said, "and it took two hundred years to complete."

Toby interrupted.

"I can just imagine the thirteenth-century project manager talking to the owner of the local brickworks: 'Hey, Thierry, I'm going to need around four million bricks. Yes, I know that's a biggish order, but you can deliver them over the next two hundred years? That's only twenty thousand a year'."

The cathedral walls were indented into small chapels surmounted by a gallery. The chapel dedicated to Sainte Cécile graphically described her history, and Yves did the translation.

Born in Rome around the year 200, so legend has it, Sainte Cécile took a vow of virginity which she maintained even after being forcibly married. But she was martyred because she converted many, including her husband, to the new Christian faith. She is now the patron saint of musicians.

The children were getting bored in the cathedral, so their parents took them to a fun fair on the other side of the square while the others stopped at one of the kerbside cafés which stretched all the way up to the old part of the town, and ordered a light lunch with wine. The families celebrated the finish of a very big weekend, and when they left two days later the château seemed to draw a sigh – perhaps of relief – that it could once again relax and doze gently in the increasing summer warmth.

5·

INTO SUMMER

BOTH Mark and Toby had bought secondhand Peugeot SUVs, which were garaged at the château so that Bernard could drive to Blagnac, the airport for Toulouse, and meet them when they arrived from London. Flying was easier than driving a thousand kilometres to and from the port of Calais if they took the ferry or the Eurotunnel.

It was now July. Mark and Pru had just picked up Chris, Diane and the children from the airport, and they were having lunch in Toulouse at a restaurant on the Place Capitole which attracted tourists who liked to dine outside in the warmer months and retained a local clientele who always preferred to eat in the elegant interior.

Chloe was sitting next to her mother on the red velour *banquette* which ran along each heavily mirrored wall and Chris and Joey sat opposite; to their left was a vacant table for two. A plump lady squeezed in next to Chloe and a small dog jumped out of her shoulder bag and settled down between them. Chloe had grown up with dogs – in her family black Labradors were *de rigeur* – and wasn't afraid of them. But she had never seen one inside a restaurant, and as she studied this one, and its owner, her blue eyes widened and her eyebrows rose.

Mark declared that in France there seemed to be no rule that a foreigner can define when it came to consistency with canines.

"We once stayed in a small hotel in the Loire valley and these visitors brought a cocker spaniel to the dining room. When our waitress politely asked the owner to remove it World War Three seemed set to break out. The owner refused, the proprietor's wife was called in, and she stated that she was unable to serve them if the dog remained. The owner said he would have to stay in the car with the dog and Madame said that would be fine by her. Eventually the dog was put in the car on its own and the owner very grumpily ate his five-course dinner. The next morning I congratulated Madame, who said *'C'est normale'.*"

They had noticed that at least one of their neighbours at the château had three dogs, none of which were desexed *(il cout trop cher)*. One was a guard dog chained up for twenty-three hours a day. Another spent its life in a small cage and a kennel, except when taken out for hunting. The third one had litters that were quickly disposed of. None of this accorded well with their Anglo sensibilities.

On the other hand, it was invariably a pleasure to be in a restaurant or other public place with French children. Usually they were well-mannered, quiet, and able to sit and eat a full meal without needing the constant distractions – paper, colouring pencils, iPads, video games and so on – which seemed to be essential for English-speaking children.

Another very noticeable and welcome difference was the way even small French children respected adults. Strangers were greeted by boys with a handshake and a *"Bonjour"* while girls would offer their cheeks or even, if you were close friends of the parents, a lip-to-lip *bisou*. If you were lucky, an English kid might give you a grunt, avoiding eye contact at all cost. It indicated to them that Anglos were more at home raising dogs than children.

***

Sarah's baby was due during the family's first summer holiday together in their new home, so she and Tom would be delayed. But her mother and father as well as sister Lucy were all expected at the château, as were the grandparents. Toby had also invited his historian friend Dr Frugier to visit for a few days in August, so they would certainly not be bored.

Life settled into a nice domestic pattern. At the start of each week Pru, and Jenny when she was there, would see how many of the family and their guests were staying, work out the communal meals, do a bit of menu planning, and make out the shopping lists. The sisters, accompanied by Alice, would do the main shopping on Tuesday. Alice was proving to be a treasure: she knew all the local retailers, recommended the best bakers and butchers, and was adept at buying supermarket items at the best prices.

One morning Tomas, the real estate agent, rang to ask if he could come over as soon as possible. He was reluctant to say why on the phone, so Mark made an appointment to see him the following afternoon.

They sat down after the formalities and Tomas got straight to the point.

"Monsieur Escott, you should know that Madame de Montfort's farmhouse is being put on the market and we were wondering whether you and Monsieur Burlington would be interested in purchasing it." he said.

"But Madame de Montfort has a life interest in the house. She told us about it," Mark said.

"You are correct about her right of tenure, Monsieur Escott, but the problem is that the property is heavily mortgaged and now, with only a small pension and what she receives from renting out the *gite*, Madame de Montfort is not even able to pay the interest on those loans. The banks have decided that they have to, what is the word, foreclose before their loss gets even bigger. Already the total debt is getting close to a million euros, and we are advising them that they cannot possibly expect to get more than five hundred thousand for the house. There is not much farmland still attached to her property either. Besides which, prices for land around here are very low unless you can build on it, and this area is designated for agricultural use. As you may know, the farmhouse has five bedrooms and a small *gite* attached. There is also the large barn which might be converted into another *gite,* perhaps two if the owner can get planning permission."

He looked at Mark and Pru questioningly. "Do you think you might be interested? I would be happy to arrange an inspection for you."

The Escotts looked at each other and both knew what the other was thinking: more money, more work, and for what? Granted, Yvette de Montfort was a good neighbour who kept to herself, and a new owner might not be so agreeable. But that sort of risk was out of their hands.

"Tomas, we appreciate your coming here to tell us this news," Mark said. "We shall have to discuss it with Pru's sister and brother-in-law. If you will give us until next Monday I will get back to you with at least a preliminary answer."

As they showed Tomas out, the park across the terrace was looking particularly scenic with dappled sunlight filtering through the trees. Tomas remarked admiringly on how they had improved the property.

"When I think back to our first meeting nearly two years ago I am *bouleversé* . . ."

"Bowled over?" Pru offered.

"Yes, bowled over with what you have done. I think old Monsieur de Montfort would be very happy to see his beloved château restored to its former glory, and more. *Au revoir Madame et Monsieur Escott, et à bientot, j'espère.*"

Pru and Mark went inside as Tomas drove off, decided they needed a drink, opened a chilled *rosé*, and went back out to the patio.

"Well, a big surprise to round off a hot day in mid-July," said Mark. "I wasn't expecting that."

"Nor I," Pru agreed. "But you know, in hindsight we might have. We knew a bit about the state of the mortgages and clearly Yvette doesn't have much cash. It must be terrible for her."

They were joined at this point by Chris and Diane returning with Chloe and Joey from the public swimming pool, where they liked to go and play with other kids. Chris had followed in his maternal grandfather's footsteps and had taken to the law: he was a successful young barrister in a commercial law practice at chambers in London's prestigious Inner Temple legal precinct. Since the acquisition of the château he had become interested in the legal aspects of owning property in France, and when his father told them of the conversation with Tomas he spoke his mind.

"Quite apart from the money, I think you should all ask yourselves whether you want to become landlords in France. I'm assuming that you don't want to run a *chambre d'hotes* or some *gites* yourselves, so you would be looking for full-time tenants for the farmhouse. There was a very interesting article in *Connexion* a few months ago which had some strong recommendations against it."

"Please summarise," Mark asked.

"Okay," Chris said. "It's like this. The main point is that the tenant-landlord relationship is heavily weighted on the side of the tenant, in particular their rights of tenure. Do you know that a tenant cannot be evicted between November and February, whatever he may have done. Failure to pay the rent will require the landlord to get a court order, and it is virtually impossible for an owner to insist that his tenant fulfils even a simple obligation like cutting the lawn or cleaning the windows. About the only way a landlord can repossess his own house fairly easily is if he can prove his need to occupy it himself. There is also a subtle suggestion that the courts tend to be even more on the side of the tenant if the landlord is a foreigner."

"And I would not want to be at the beck and call of a tenant who is also our next-door neighbour," Pru said. "That's too much potential for conflict."

"Too right," Diane said.

"Then there's the money," Mark said. "I'm not saying we spent too much on buying and doing up the château but we did spend a lot, and with that experience behind us I'm sure buying and renovating Yvette's place wouldn't show us any change out of a million euros. I'll call Toby and tell him that our recommendation is a no."

Toby was in complete agreement and the decision was made. That it turned out to be a momentous one would only be revealed much later.

***

Lucy was the next one to arrive. After finishing her degree in history at University College London and attending the graduation ceremony in late June she had some free time before taking job interviews, and was aiming for a career in marketing.

Yves met her at the airport. They had not seen each other since the weekend of the commune's fete but had kept in contact through Facebook and an occasional phone call. Yves suggested a couple of nights in the Pyrenees before she met up with her family and booked them into a *chambre d'hotes* in a village called Esparros, just south of Lannemezan. It overlooked a valley encompassing the Foret de Baronnies, up to the Pic du Midi, which at nearly twenty-five hundred metres was the highest point in the mountain range.

They arrived at six-thirty in the evening and were shown to their room by a charming middle-aged woman who told them dinner would be served in an hour, but if they felt like an aperitif beforehand she and her husband would be happy to oblige. Their room was spacious, with a double bed and a big window opening onto a small balcony which gave a wonderful view of the Pic. Lucy kissed Yves and murmured "Thank you."

They went downstairs and met the hosts, Madame and Monsieur Lacroix, who offered them a choice of *pastis* or sweet white wine. They chose the *pastis*. Dinner was served by Madame, a veritable feast. The entrée was *gesiers* salad, duck gizzards, a local gourmet dish, followed by a *faux filet* in red wine sauce with potatoes and courgettes, accompanied by a light red from a local vineyard. To Madame's disappointment they declined the dessert.

After dinner, Lucy and Yves sat on their balcony, holding hands and watching the moon rise. Large and almost orange, it was lighting up the mountains and being reflected off the north face of the Pic where there were still traces of snow. It was impossible for Lucy to think of anywhere more romantic.

"Let's go to bed," she said as she stood up, still holding Yves' hand.

"If we do . . . it . . . it will be my first time," he said, embarrassed.

Lucy gave him a gentle hug.

"Don't worry, we'll be fine," she reassured him. "Let's just take our clothes off."

When they awoke next morning, wrapped in contentment, the sun was shining on the Pic and it seemed to be smiling down on them too.

With a full day to themselves and another night booked at the Lacroix, they decided after a coffee and *tartine* breakfast to drive through the valley and take the winding road up into the mountains. It was stunning. After Bagneres de Bigorre they reached La Mongie and took the chairlift to the Pic, where they could look out over the whole range of the Pyrenees. The weather was perfect, visibility high, and they capped off the experience with a tour of the fascinating exhibition in the old observatory nearly three thousand metres above sea level.

That evening at the Lacroix house, dinner was an *entrée* of homegrown tomatoes topped with mozzarella cheese and herbs, and another local favourite: *cassoulet* with *confit de canard,* sausage and beans baked in a casserole. It was tasty, if a little heavy for a warm evening.

In the morning they made an early start to see Yves' mother, who had invited Lucy to lunch to meet her. Madame Marty was in her mid-fifties and still an extremely attractive woman. She greeted Lucy warmly and gave her son a big hug too, as well as a mildly enquiring smile. He would be interrogated later!

Also present was Yves' cousin, Angelique Bardou, a woman in her mid-thirties who was a primary school teacher, like Lucy's mother.

"I must meet your mother," Angelique said, "and if she would like to, I could arrange for her to visit our local school next term.

I am only teaching part-time as I have two young daughters but I hope to be back full-time next year."

So it was arranged that Angelique would bring her girls to the château and meet Jenny next week.

Yves helped his mother prepare and serve lunch, a big platter of *charcuterie*. He explained to Lucy that it was a family tradition: once a year, when the extended Bardou family gathered, at least two pigs would be slaughtered and everyone would be given a task. This year Yves had been promoted, responsible for dividing up the carcasses, deciding who should make the different sorts of sausages, and which meat should be cured or salted.

"After all, I am training to be a chef," he declared proudly.

When the meal was cleared away, Yves asked his mother for permission to take Lucy home to the château before he returned to Toulouse, as he was working the next day. Lucy thanked Madame Marty for the lunch, promised Angelique that she would speak to her mother about getting together, and said *au revoir*.

Their farewell kiss at the entrance to the château was warm but brief. Yves told Lucy he was in love with her, and she said, "I know . . . and please let me know when I can be with you again." Yves drove off, partly happy and partly sad.

Toby and Jenny were waiting for Lucy as she walked down the driveway carrying her overnight bag.

"So, are we in love?" asked her father, never one to be shy with a direct question.

"Toby!" said Jenny sharply. "Give the girl a chance to sit down. Darling, it's so nice to see you and you look so lovely. Ignore your father and just tell us about all the nice places you've been to and the nice things you've done . . . well some of them anyway."

Lucy gave them an edited version of the past three days.

55

"Yes, I am in love. He is a delightful, thoughtful and caring person, and now that I've met his mother I can see why. We hope to see much more of each other during the summer. I also met his cousin and she's lovely too. She's a primary school teacher too, Mum, and I've invited her to come over to meet you next week. She'll probably bring her two little girls with her. I hope that's okay."

"You seem to have the whole family sorted out," her Dad said. "And I'm sure we shall love meeting them too, shall we not, Jenny?"

***

Angelique and her daughters, Marianne and Mathilde, arrived just after midday the following Tuesday and were greeted by everyone staying at the château. After having a glass of sauvignon blanc together, the Escott family departed and left Lucy and her parents alone on the terrace with their guests while Alice served lunch.

The little girls were perfectly behaved, but four-year-old Mathilde didn't greet them with a *bisou,* the way they now normally expected, and avoided eye contact. Her mother had brought a rug and some toys, and sat Mathilde on the grass near them.

"She will play with those toys for hours, always the same game," Angelique said. "And I hope you don't mind, but I have brought some food for her as she is very restrictive in what she will eat."

Marianne, nearly eight, was quite different. She joined in the adults' conversation and ate the meal, cold zucchini soup and prawn salad. The talk was mostly about primary education and the differences between their two countries, and Jenny accepted the invitation to visit the local school with Angelique next term. She offered to take a class and put together an audiovisual presentation, perhaps on the British Royal Family.

Angelique was delighted. "That will be much appreciated, and the children do know a bit about the princes. In fact, we French people secretly envy the British for having a monarchy – but don't tell anyone I said that!"

Lucy took Marianne to the kitchen to see if Pru would care to join them, and Jenny asked Angelique a question as they skipped away.

"Excuse my asking this, Angelique, but we both have a lot of experience with young children and it seems that Mathilde may have a problem. Have you had any diagnosis?"

Angelique stared at Jenny before answering.

"You are of course quite right, Jenny. Mathilde does have problems. We first noticed them when she was about eighteen months old. Very little attempt at speech and even less non-verbal communication. She rarely smiles or laughs and she does not seem to want physical affection. Her habits, like her eating, are very restricted, and her patterns of behaviour are repetitive and limited."

Pru arrived a few seconds later and Lucy took Marianne for a swim as Angelique continued.

"We think she has some degree of autism, but we are fearful of taking professional advice."

"Why is that?" asked Pru, who had seen Mathilde at play before lunch.

"Because autistic children are frequently removed from their parents. In France, many, probably most psychoanalysts, still believe that autism is the child's reaction to a lack of love from their parents, particularly the mother."

"Ah, the refrigerator mother syndrome," said Pru. "That old

myth. It's been abandoned by almost every country in the world for at least thirty years now but still lives on in France. Oh dear."

"Exactly. But the whole system here is predicated on people being 'normal'. A child showing 'differences' may be denied an ordinary education, and very little help is given in trying to integrate them into a regular school. In the worst cases they may be put into institutions where the treatment can be awful. Do you know the French word *packing*? It means that extreme and violent cases may be literally tied up in cold, wet sheets, a practice which has been condemned by the European Court of Human Rights but still goes on."

"How is it possible that France is still holding on to these archaic and abusive views and practices?" Jenny asked.

"Post-Freudian psychoanalysis still has a major voice here, and we have suffered a great deal from the teachings of Bruno Bettelheim, who, as I'm sure you know, preached that autism was caused by psychological damage. He and his followers said they had often observed in clinical conditions a lack of affection on the part of the mother towards an autistic child."

Pru countered. "And sometimes that may be the *effect* on the mother of having a child who displays little or no emotion towards her, rather than the *cause* of the child's problem. Exactly the opposite way round to Bettelheim's theories. As for him, he was eventually found to be a complete fraud who emigrated from Austria with forged documents, including all his degrees and diplomas. He held some very prestigious positions in America and influenced a whole generation of thought and research into various conditions, including schizophrenia, as well as autism, which is now generally accepted as being a problem of neurological development."

Jenny re-entered the conversation.

"Pru is a music therapist and she still practices in London. Do you have any suggestions, Pru?"

"Sometimes we can make some enhancements to the lives of people with these difficulties," Pru said. "I would need to sit with Mathilde and make a thorough assessment of her first. One of my colleagues is coming to stay for a few days in August and it would be better for the two of us to do it. That's if you wanted us to, of course."

"That would be wonderful," said Angelique, and so it was arranged.

***

Towards the end of July, Tomas rang again to say that a serious offer for Yvette's farmhouse had been received from a married couple with two teenage children in Toulouse.

Mark followed up this news with a phone call and then a visit to the mayor, who confirmed that a sale looked likely.

"They seem a nice family, Mark. The parents, Monsieur and Madame LeBlanc, are probably forty years of age. They have enquired about the possibility of converting the big old barn into two *gites* and I have told them that they would probably get authorisation. Nothing for you to worry about, I assure you."

"Well that's good to know. Could you keep me informed as things develop?" Mark asked.

"Of course. And, as you will remember, it will probably take two to three months before the purchase is finalised."

"Thank you, Michel. When you see Monsieur LeBlanc, can you tell him that we would like to meet him and his family and that they will be very welcome to visit the château."

On that they parted. Mark went home, and the days got longer and hotter as the end of the month approached.

6.

SOME HOT AUGUST NIGHTS

AS THE summer heat intensified the château seemed to snuggle down. Following local practice, the shutters on the sunny side facing south were closed during the day to keep it cool, and the house looked as if it were gently sleeping.

Most mornings were spent doing chores and shopping. In the shade of the plane trees, lunch would be prepared by Pru or Jenny and Alice, and afterwards the children swam in the pool and played backgammon while the oldies took a siesta.

August would see a big influx of visitors, first the grandparents, Sir Robert and Lady Ann Williams. While proud of their grandfather, the families showed him no great deference. He was affectionately and universally known as the "Old Bastard", or the OB, and tickled pink by the nickname. A life in the law had seen him rise through the ranks of criminal barristers until he was appointed a judge of the Crown Court and the Court of Appeal, before being knighted for services to jurisprudence. He was well known for handing out blistering rebukes to barristers he felt were deliberately misleading a jury or paying insufficient respect to the court whose honour he had sworn to uphold. Hence the OB sobriquet, which could be softened to "Old Bob" to avoid further censure if an indignant or humiliated young barrister was overheard being critical of "My Lord".

Lady Ann was a wife and mother and a born carer, first for her husband, then her daughters, now for her grandchildren. She had taken a degree in nursing when her girls were in their teens, and although never actually employed she took on numerous voluntary jobs with some of the larger London hospitals. She was a quiet lady and an invaluable asset to her outspoken husband.

This was Robert and Ann's first visit to the château and they were immediately entranced, ensconced in the largest guest bedroom at the rear, which was cooler, quieter, and looked out over the poplars and sweeping lawns that stretched away to the river. Beyond were fields of wheat and sunflowers climbing gently towards another tiny commune. "Bloody magic" was the OB's comment.

They were staying for three weeks, happy to get up late, enjoy a coffee and a *pain au raisin* with whomever was in the kitchen, then go outside and find deckchairs in the shade.

Toby had also invited Dr Frugier and he was the next to arrive. Although a lot younger than the OB, they hit it off and were soon immersed in conversation over early evening drinks.

"I gather you're not here to give medical advice, Dr Frugier," Sir Robert said matter of factly.

"Definitely not, Sir Robert. My speciality is history, French history in particular. That is one reason why it is such a pleasure and an honour to be invited to this wonderful old house, but also of course to meet your family. And please call me Alain."

"I shall, if you call me Robert. I've always been a huge fan of France. My first visit was with a school party back in 1950. We went to some of the First World War graveyards in the north and then to Paris. That was an experience for young lads. Not like London and the other British cities which were being rebuilt after the Second World War. Here they hadn't even cleared up the war damage in some places, and Paris was dirty. Most of the buildings hadn't been cleaned for years, and the streets . . . well, you certainly watched where you were walking. But I loved it. I remember Notre Dame, going up the bell towers. I bought a little gargoyle as a present for my mother."

"You are quite right, Robert. Paris only started to clean itself up in the late fifties and sixties when de Gaulle was in power again. The years before that were not good for us. Firstly the whole business of getting the country together again in 1944 with a provisional government for two years, and then the Fourth Republic, which was about as hopeless as the Third had been before the war. And then the troubles in Algeria which tore France and the French people apart. I was only a boy, but I remember much of that decade and it was terrible."

Robert jumped in.

"I was lucky because my father had friends in Paris and they would often invite me to stay with them. One thing I've never quite understood, Alain, is why France was the only major country in Europe to agree on an armistice with the Germans, which seems to have gained it very little except a token government in Vichy."

"Well, it is certainly a complicated subject and one that is still not openly discussed in our school curriculum. Three factors made Vichy possible. The first was the terrible fear in most of the population that another major war would be fought on their soil. Secondly, the fear of a communist-inspired revolution and takeover. And then the wish that a better constitution could be created. When Marshall Pétain offered safety from the first two, and said he would gain a good post-war deal for France from the

Nazis, his offer was readily accepted by the vast majority of the population."

"The vast majority? Really? Isn't the post-war belief that only a relatively small number of the population were collaborators?"

"Yes, but what exactly is collaboration? Certainly the number of French people actively participating in the worst acts of the Nazis – the rounding-up and deportation of Jews for instance – was relatively small. But is not passive acquiescence a form of collaboration? In 1940, Pétain promised that his negotiations would bring several specific concessions from the Germans. Firstly, the release and repatriation of French prisoners of war. There were over a million of them. Secondly, that the costs of occupation would be reduced. These were a huge drain on the government revenues. Thirdly, that the French colonies in Africa would be protected from takeover by the British. And lastly, that when either the Germans had won the war or negotiated a peace with the British, France would be restored to a significant place in the new Europe. In return, Pétain promised the Nazis that he could maintain peaceful control over the unoccupied part of France – Vichy – and said he would be happy to recruit French labour to go to work in the German factories."

"And did the Germans accept these proposals?"

"Not one of them. The top Nazi leadership was not having any of it. Hitler hated France and wanted to exact *revanche*, revenge, for 1918. During the four years of occupation things got worse. Take the situation of the prisoners of war. They were only released under specific conditions, one of which was that one POW could be released for every five workers volunteering, or being sent, to factories in Germany to work in appalling conditions. From mid-1942, when the Germans occupied Vichy, only Pierre Laval, who was their puppet, ever got to speak to the senior Nazis. He agreed to assist them in rounding up and

63

deporting Jews, to start with only foreign ones, mostly refugees, and then French nationals as well. But even in the first half of 1944 the thing most people in France feared was an Allied invasion, and Pétain and his diplomats were still trying to persuade the Americans to talk peace terms."

"So how did the big upsurge in the Resistance movement come about?" the OB asked.

"Well, from 1942 onwards, yes, there was an increase in the membership of the Resistance. But a lot of them were young men in danger of being sent to Germany, so they took to hiding out in the hills. You have to remember that the Nazis and later the *Milice,* the Vichy's own paramilitaries, took savage reprisals against civilians for acts of violence against the German military, so in a way it was not surprising that the majority did not actively support the Resistance. But then came the Allied invasion in Normandy and the Germans were being pushed back. By August of 1944 General de Gaulle was in Paris and, surprise surprise, everyone wanted to be on the winning side. Suddenly everyone had been secret supporters of the Resistance. The obvious collaborators were punished, many thousands by summary execution, but most of the Vichy leaders went to trial. Many received prison sentences but only a few were given the death penalty."

"Thank you," said Robert. "That was most enlightening, and I would like to return to that topic again. Now I think they're calling us to dinner."

Next day the mayor telephoned Mark, saying, "Would it be possible to come and see you? I have something to ask you."

"Delighted," said Mark, and twenty minutes later Michel Ricard parked his Renault on the terrace. They shook hands and Mark offered him a drink.

"Thank you, a small glass of beer would be very welcome."

They sat down and clinked glasses to *"a votre santé"*.

"So what can I do for you?" Mark asked after they had taken a long draught.

"This is unusual, and please understand I will not be offended if you say no to what I am going to ask. We have, at the moment, Christian de Montfort and his wife Suzanne staying with us, and of course we discuss the commune, and what I think you call the good old times. I have told Christian what a marvellous renovation you have made and, well, he asked me if I thought you might let them see it. I know you have many of your family and friends here for the summer but Christian would not, I think, be too intrusive, and I would be happy to escort them if you wished".

Mark went silent, wondering what was the real reason behind the request.

"Well, that does come as a surprise," he said slowly. "I'm at a bit of a loss for a quick response. I think I'd better ask my brother-in-law and our wives. What if I do that at lunchtime and call you this afternoon?"

"Perfect," Michel said, finishing his beer and taking his leave.

Mark broached the subject over lunch as the main course of *daurade*, sea bass steamed in alufoil with slivers of vegetables, was served. Not unexpectedly, the OB was the first to respond.

"Love to meet the son of a major collaborator. Great idea, Mark."

Alain Frugier could not stop himself from laughing.

"But never convicted, Robert. You had better watch your step, *mon vieux!* He's a politician and probably highly sensitive of his dignity."

Everyone joined in the laughter.

"I'd be happy to meet them and offer them an *apero* after the tour," Pru volunteered.

"Good idea," said her sister, "but nothing too fancy. An hour here one evening should be enough."

They all agreed and Mark was tasked with setting up the visit.

At six p.m. two days later Michel Ricard drove up to the house and Mark and Toby greeted Madame and Monsieur de Montfort, before introducing them to the rest of the family and Dr Frugier. The late afternoon sun was partly obscured by a cloud and a shadow had fallen over the building. It almost looked as if the château was scowling.

Christian appeared to be relaxed and his wife seemed warm and friendly. Pru and Jenny, who could both by now speak passably good French, started their tour of the house straight away, on the ground floor. Christian delighted in remembrance of his formative years here as they went from room to room.

"Ah, this is where my mother had her piano and we had such happy times learning to sing the traditional songs of this region," he said in one room. And in another, "Here mother would do her sewing. We were not very well off for money, you understand, and she would mend our clothes." The new kitchen was a huge surprise. "*Mon Dieu!* To think that when we lived here we had animals in this room. *Formidable.*" But when they went upstairs Christian was speechless.

"You have made a wonderful renovation," he eventually managed to say. "I cannot believe how beautiful the château has become after so many years of neglect and decline. I am very happy for the château and also for you. *Mes félicitations.*"

Out in the garden Christian remarked favourably on the new plantings and complimented Mark on the way the parkland was so well ordered.

"We could never afford gardeners," he said. "This is superb. My father would have been so happy to see it as it must have been in his youth."

Alice appeared with a bottle of champagne and Mark poured their guests a glass.

"We are happy to welcome you to your old home," he said to Christian. "It must hold many happy memories for you. Maybe some sad ones too?"

"That is very true," said Christian. "I'm sure you know that my father's death caused a great schism in our family. Unfortunately, my brother and I could not agree on a fair division of his estate and my mother took the side of my brother. I have not seen her for many years, but I hear that she has to sell the farmhouse and will soon be moving away from the place which has been her home for more than fifty years. That is sad, but frankly, if she and my brother had been more reasonable none of this would have happened."

Christian turned to Alain. "Doctor Frugier, I know your name and I think you may be a writer?"

"I am firstly an historian, *Monsieur,* but yes, I have written a few books on aspects of French history."

"Including one, I think, on the German occupation of France? I seem to recall that you were not too kind about my late father."

"*Monsieur*, I have spent many years researching historical documents – French, German and many others – and then I write the facts that have been revealed to me. That is what I believe good historians should do, not paint a picture which is more acceptable but distorts the truth."

"Ah, the truth. There are some truths that depend on through whose eyes they are seen, I believe."

The Old Bastard could not be restrained.

"Monsieur de Montfort," he said. "It has been my privilege, and occasionally my pleasure, to sit on the bench of one of the highest courts in the United Kingdom, where we attempted to discover if not always the truth at least the most likely reasons which led to particular events. It usually came down to choice: at a certain moment in time a person is faced with a choice. Which way to go? Once that choice is taken the next steps are often irrevocable. Sometimes that choice is extremely difficult. On the one hand, there appear to be some practical advantages, but sometimes, on the other hand, there is a moral balance sheet which must be carefully considered. From what I understand, in 1940 Marshall Pétain saw many potentially positive aspects of an armistice with Germany and decided to ignore the moral downside, and many Frenchmen followed him."

"I could not have put it better myself," said Alain.

"I see you have convicted my father already," said Christian sarcastically. "Fortunately his jury did not agree with you. Anyway, we must thank you for your hospitality and leave. I'm sure it is time for your dinner. *Au revoir* and enjoy the rest of the summer."

Christian and his wife, who hadn't spoken a word, handed Mark the half-empty champagne glasses, walked to their car, and drove off with Michel Ricard, who had also stayed out of the conversation.

"What do you make of that?" Mark asked no one in particular.

"I think that bugger's full of envy and resentment," the OB said. "Keep an eye on him, Mark. And now let's talk some more about me."

They laughed and relaxed. The sun had come out of the cloud now and the house seemed almost to be laughing with them.

***

A few days later the mayor called again.

"Sorry to disturb you," he said to Mark, "but I have suggested to the family LeBlanc that they should meet you. They are getting very near to signing the *compromis de vente* and are hoping that the sale of the farm will be completed before Christmas."

"We'd be delighted," Mark said. "Please tell them that we do not have any plans for the next few days."

The mayor rang back to say the LeBlancs would come to the château the following morning. They were on holiday too, as most of France seemed to be.

Just before eleven they arrived in a not overly expensive Citroen and introduced themselves: father Hervé, mother Anne-Marie, thirteen-year-old daughter Brigitte and her ten-year-old brother Virgil. Pru and Jenny ushered them into the château and offered cool drinks, which they politely refused.

"We do not wish to take up too much of your time," said Hervé LeBlanc. "Merely to introduce ourselves to the family who will, we hope, very soon become our neighbours. You probably know that the papers are nearly ready to be signed, but this is August and this is France, so it will probably be well into September before things start moving again. And the mayor tells us that you will probably be going back to England at the end of this month."

"Yes," said Mark. "But we will give you our contact details so you can keep us informed of your progress."

Chris joined in. "If I may ask, Monsieur LeBlanc, do you have any major *clauses suspensives* in the draft *compromis*? I'm thinking here of requirements by you for building authorisations or major alterations to the property. Those are clauses which must be fulfilled for the sale to take place," he added for the benefit of his family.

"Yes we do," replied LeBlanc, "but nothing I think which will affect yourselves. We wish to have permission to put in a

69

swimming pool, as you have done I believe, and we also wish to convert the barn at the rear of the farm into a *gite*. We do not think there will be a problem, but it is best to know."

"Thank you," Chris said. "We shall be interested to hear your progress. Would you like us to show you around the château?"

The LeBlancs nodded enthusiastically, and when the tour was completed they all sat down in the garden.

"We currently live near Toulouse," Anne-Marie LeBlanc said, "and we both work in companies contracted to Airbus. Hervé is an engineer specialising in heat-resistant materials and I am a programmer. I work in the area of providing data to the flight crews. We enjoy our jobs but we are hoping to reduce our hours so we can spend more time here eventually. We hope also that when they are a little older Brigitte and Virgil will be able to attend schools in this area. We are told that there are some very good ones."

"Well, one person we can introduce you to to talk about schools is young Madame Bardou, who is a teacher and lives in the village," said Pru. "She is very nice and we already know her quite well."

"Thank you, I would like that," Anne-Marie replied. "And now I think we should not take up any more of your holiday time. We are very happy to have met you and to see the château, and we hope that we shall soon be neighbours."

"Well we're certainly getting to know the locals," said Toby as the LeBlancs' car disappeared up the driveway. "And one thing we ought to do before we leave is have another chat with the mayor about those planning permissions LeBlanc mentioned. We should try to see the one for the conversion of the barn. It's a pretty big building and I'd like to know if it's going to affect our peace and quiet."

"Good point, Toby," Chris said. "And I'll do a bit more

research on what can and can't be done in an area like this. We know it's zoned agricultural, but there is obviously a certain amount of latitude for creating accommodation for tourists from all those ads you see for *gites* and *chambres d'hotes*."

***

By mid-August the temperatures were well into the thirties, although the nights were reasonably cool. In the daytime the family and their guests gravitated to the shade of the trees or the swimming pool. In the afternoon heat buzzing cicadas could be heard, but as dusk fell they quietened down to a low purring sound – or was that a noise the house was making?

Alain Frugier was leaving the next day, so they gathered that evening for a farewell dinner. He thanked the family and raised his glass in a toast: *"A la santé de la famille de Sir Robert and Lady Ann et merci à tous."*

The families responded and the OB spoke up.

"Alain, I cannot tell you what a pleasure it has been to have met you and to hear your views on all sorts of things. You have reinforced my love for France and its people, although I still do not fully understand the national psyche. On the one hand you are incredibly conservative, and on the other you maintain the strict separation of church and state, which is not a bad thing to my mind. And then you have a bureaucracy which is mind-numbingly inefficient and frustrating. But perhaps these are all features of your resistance to change. Your views, sir?"

Alain smiled. "To us," he replied, "the Revolution was the key instance in our history when so much was changed, some things for the better, others not. But we have hung on to 1789 and the years of Napoleon, when we became a truly great power with new ideas and institutions, and we tend to fear changing anything that we have inherited from those days in case the whole fabric of our society starts to crumble. I do not think we are cowards in a physical sense, but we do dread change. That is why so many of our laws and customs date back to that era, some two hundred years ago. But be fair to us, Robert. You English also love your traditions: your Royal family, your ceremonials, your lack of a formal constitution. Plus, you have not had a revolution since the seventeenth century and you, in contrast to us French, very quickly decided that it was a great mistake."

"Come on, Robert," Toby said. "We can tell that you are about to let us know all about seeing history through old eyes. Please entertain and enlighten us."

There was a barely suppressed laugh around the table.

"One thing you will learn, my dear son-in-law," said Robert, rising to the bait, "should you be so privileged to live as long as I have, is that there are no eternal truths. Each generation sees very similar situations from a different perspective. Were England now to find itself in the situation, say, of France in 1940, it might well concede victory to an overwhelming power, whereas we have spent the last seventy-five years congratulating ourselves on saving the world. But I am getting old and boring – do not agree too quickly, Toby – so I will only say that being of a considerable age does not necessarily confer wisdom, merely experience. And I cannot but say that getting older is no great pleasure in itself. Not only does the body start to give up some of its functions, so does the mind. These days it is a bonus for me to go into a room and remember why."

***

Pru's friend and colleague from London, Nicole Price, arrived towards the end of the month and Angelique Bardou was invited to bring Mathilde to the château so the two music therapists could make an assessment of her condition and see whether they could help her.

They spent nearly two hours talking, singing and playing simple tunes on the piano with the little girl, rarely eliciting a response. She seemed reasonably happy – at least she didn't cry or become emotional – but hardly smiled. They concluded that Mathilde was suffering from a developmental delay which was probably the cause of her speech difficulties.

Nicole opened the conversation with Angelique.

"We think that this delay in her intellectual development might be combined with a sense that her sister is always the focus of attention. Not jealousy exactly, but an awareness that Mathilde falls short of her sister in social interaction. That's causing a lack of confidence, which is driving her towards more introverted behaviour. We would like to help her in addressing the issues that are stemming from this, things like her motor movement and communication skills and self-confidence. We think you will see an improvement."

"The problem is one of geography," Pru said. "Mathilde is here and we shall soon be going back to London. But we can offer one possible solution."

"And what might that might that be?" Angelique said. "I would be prepared to do almost anything for Mathilde because I feel like I have lost her."

"Well," said Nicole, "we suggest that you bring Mathilde to London. We would develop a program for her at our music therapy centre for a two-week period, and expect to make some progress."

"You would both be welcome to stay with us," Pru said, "but we might have something better to suggest. We have a friend,

Nancy, and she is a widow with no children of her own, which is her greatest sadness. But now she is like a perfect grandmother, and you and Mathilde would love her. If Mathilde was happy at Nancy's she could stay on when you went home, or come to London more often for therapy."

"It sounds almost to be good to be true," said Angelique, with tears in her eyes.

***

Yves had accepted the family's invitation to stay at the château overnight from time to time, but late in August he had a few days' leave and wanted to take another trip with Lucy.

Knowing that the holiday traffic in the south would be heavy until the end of the month, he suggested heading north to Rocamadour in the valley of the Dordogne. He found another *chambres d'hote* in a neighbouring village and they set off.

The three-hour drive brought them to a stunning sight when the village came into view: a nesting eagle, sitting above a canyon. As they climbed the two hundred and sixteen steps up to the village, Yves explained that this was a sacred site for hundreds of years for pilgrims from all over Europe who wanted to pray and be comforted by the statue in the church of Notre Dame – the carved-timber Black Virgin, whose history was lost in time.

As they stood holding hands and taking in the spectacular countryside below Lucy was captivated.

"It's just wonderful," she breathed. "You and the view."

Once again Yves had picked an excellent place to stay. The evening meal was taken with an older couple from England who spoke little French, which gave Lucy the opportunity of translating the dishes. It was simple fare: the main course was a hearty vegetarian casserole with couscous. When the plates were cleared away, Yves suggested a walk in the moonlight and they said goodnight to their fellow guests.

They stopped to lean on a stone wall and look out over undulating meadows that stretched to the horizon under the limitless sky. Yves turned to Lucy and took her hands

"I love you very much, Lucy," he declared. "I know I am not in a position to ask you to marry me as I cannot support myself much less the two of us, but I hope to one day. For the moment, I hope you may accept a small token of that love."

She looked into his eyes as he took something from his shirt pocket that glittered in the starlight.

"It is a *bague d'amitié* – a ring of friendship," he said, sliding the ring carefully on her fourth finger. It fitted perfectly.

Lucy looked at their hands and tears welled up as she kissed him tenderly.

"It is lovely, Yves," she said. "Thank you. I could not be happier. We shall find a way to be together all the time. *Je t'aime* . . . very, very much."

***

There was one more hot night left in August, and it was a scorcher.

The mayor had invited Mark and Pru – the rest of the family having returned to London – together with his deputies, some prominent landowners and their wives to an *apero* at the Ricards' home to celebrate the *rentrée*, the return to school. The Escotts arrived at seven p.m. and were greeted by Michel and Adilah. The mayor embraced Pru and ushered her off to the sitting room and courtyard where the other guests were gathered. Adilah then walked up to Mark, put her arms round his neck and kissed him. Not the usual left-cheek, right-cheek peck but full-on lips with passionate intensity.

"I adore you, Mark," she sighed in his ear as she let him go. Mark was stunned into silence and followed her outside.

The evening passed without further incident. The mayor reinforced his advice that the family living in the Château du Moulin should not worry about the LeBlancs' planning application, and Mark ensured that Pru was holding his arm when they said *adieu*. He decided not to mention the encounter with Adilah.

Then it was time to pack up after spending a marvellous month in perfect weather at the château, which was proving to be even more comfortable to live in than they had imagined. As they left the next morning, Mark and Pru looked back and said *"Merci et au revoir"*, and thought they heard "à *bientot*" in return.

7.

THE BOMBSHELL

LATE in November, Mark received a call from France from Jean-Claude Bardou, the son of Jeanne, whom he had met briefly at one of the commune fetes.

"Monsieur Escott, excuse me if I am disturbing you, but I have something to tell you which I think you will find important."

"Not at all. Please go on, Jean-Claude," Mark said.

"Thank you. It concerns your neighbours. We have learned yesterday that the family LeBlanc have been granted planning authorisation, and today I went to the *Mairie* to see exactly what they are intending to do. Monsieur, I think you will be shocked. They are planning to turn the farm into a *salle d'accueil*, a reception centre for marriages and events for large numbers of people. This is a complete change of usage, but the mayor has granted it."

"*What?* Do we have an opportunity to appeal against this?" Mark asked in shock.

"I believe so, but you may have to act fast. I would with respect suggest that you come over here very soon and consult with your lawyer. You may have only a few days."

"Thank you, Jean-Claude," said Mark, and he was on the first plane to Toulouse the next morning.

Bernard picked him up at the airport and they drove straight to the château. As they passed Yvette's farm he saw a notice pinned to a tree by the gate, and after stopping the car he walked back to read it. There was official notification of the planning authorisation but little detail. He would have to wait until the *Mairie* reopened that afternoon.

The *Mairie* had only one staffer, a young woman, and her time was shared by two communes. She recognised Mark and greeted him politely, guessing what had caused his unexpected arrival without giving her thoughts away.

"Bonjour, Monsieur Escott, how may I help you?"

Mark asked to see the planning authorisation in full, with all the details. It was several pages long, and he read it with alarm. The mayor had not only granted permission for the LeBlancs to convert their barn into two *gites* and install a swimming pool, but also to convert and extend the farmhouse into a reception area seating one hundred people. The extension included an accessible flat roof area, six extra bedrooms and bathrooms – and parking for up to fifty vehicles.

Mark had been blindsided enough times during his career in the music business to know that he had to fight back fast against a strike like this, an outrageous attempt at a development coup. Armed with a copy of all the relevant papers, which included an architect's plans, he left the *Mairie* and phoned the *notaire* who had handled the purchase of the château.

"Monsieur Escott, you have need not of me but of an *avocat* experienced in this area," the *notaire* informed him. "I am frequently in touch with the best in south-west France. His name is Maitre Louis Tournier and his chambers are not far from mine here in Toulouse. I will give you his telephone number and immediately call him and explain the situation and request that he calls you without delay. You will like him. He is somewhat, shall I say *exubérant*, but he has a fine brain, much experience, and as a bonus he speaks good English. But please keep in touch with me."

The call from Maitre Tournier came within the hour and Mark was booked in for an appointment at eleven-thirty the next day.

The *avocat* was on the short side and quite rotund, but he exuded self-confidence and a sense of humour on meeting his new client.

"So, Monsieur Escott – or may I call you Mark from *le debut*, and you should call me Louis – you are yet another foreigner who falls in love with *la belle France* only to discover that many, perhaps most, Frenchmen are self-serving and deceitful. Fortunately we have ways of combating these people, but they are almost always – how do you say? – long-winded, tiresome, and expensive. So I must hope that you have patience, endurance, and most importantly, a fat cheque book."

"Well that summed things up," Mark chuckled. "Thank you, Louis, and you must certainly call me Mark. I believe Maitre Buffard has told you in general of our concerns, and I have a copy of the full authorisation which has been given to our neighbours by our mayor. But before you look at that I want to make two things clear. The first is that such a development would wreck our enjoyment of our property. And secondly, right up to September the mayor was personally assuring us that we had nothing to worry about as the application was merely for two *gites* and a swimming pool. Nobody has ever mentioned this big reception centre or six more bedrooms, let alone parking for fifty cars. As for the qualities you say we shall need, we have demonstrated all three in getting the château renovated, and I am happy to leave a cheque with you now."

"Thank you, Mark. You did well to see me so quickly because the time for lodging an appeal is rapidly disappearing. If it is possible, I would like to go through these papers right away and see you again this afternoon at, say, fourteen hundred hours?"

"Perfect, Louis."

Mark thought he deserved a decent early lunch and went to Le Bibent, where he ate *foie gras* and *cassoulet* enhanced by a half bottle of a favoured Bordeaux.

On reconvening, Louis detailed his response to the development proposal.

"Well, all is certainly not lost, my friend, but there is much to do and no time to waste. Unless your mayor can be persuaded to cancel the authorisation – and that seems to me unlikely at this stage as he will incur the wrath of the LeBlanc family – we shall have to go to the appropriate tribunal that decides such matters. This is done by the interested parties writing formal submissions, copies of which they exchange. I will start this process immediately by drafting our objections in detail, but our main line of attack will be to point out the flagrant change of usage, which I cannot believe has been granted by the appropriate authorities, from agricultural to effectively a commercial enterprise. I will send you a copy by email by tomorrow night and will appreciate your comments within twenty-four hours. Then I will lodge our submission and we shall see how your mayor responds. Is that agreeable to you?"

"It is, Louis," Mark said. "I am already feeling better than I have for forty-eight hours. I shall get back to you very quickly. One question though. Do you think I should see the mayor before or after your submission has been copied to him? I really feel that I should be showing him how I feel."

"That is really up to you, but on balance I would recommend

you wait until after he has received my letter, when he will probably also have appointed an *avocat* to defend his position."

"Then I shall be guided by you and go back to London early tomorrow to brief my brother-in-law and our wives, and we can review your draft together."

Mark handed over a cheque for two thousand euros and headed off.

Back in London he called a family meeting, and Toby, Jenny, Chris and Diane joined him and Pru at their house the next day over tea and lemon cupcake, one of Pru's specialities.

Mark had circulated the mayor's authorisation, so he began.

"I don't think I need to explain what the LeBlancs have permission to do. Suffice to say that their plans would wreck our peaceful enjoyment of the château and heavens knows what it would do to the value of the property – and I mean to get advice on that. So it seems that we have no alternative but to fight this in every way possible. I've received Louis Tournier's proposed response, and he would like our comments and hopefully our permission to proceed by this evening."

He handed out copies of the *avocat's* draft submission.

"You will see," Mark continued, "that his objections fall into three main categories. His submission is twelve pages long, so there's a lot to get through, but we have to check everything. First and perhaps most important is the question of usage. Louis points out that the farmhouse is classified as agricultural in an area which does include a small number of residential properties, but nothing that could be remotely described as commercial. He has asked the mayor for the evidence of consent from various departments and authorities, including the Department of Agriculture and the local Chamber of Commerce. He also raises the question of the effect of this type of commercial venture on the farming community. For instance, will the LeBlancs be permitted to tell a farmer that he cannot use his tractor – that is to say, make a noise – if they are about to host a wedding reception?"

"We have to remember that some communes are pushing for commercial redevelopment and maybe ours is one of them," Chris suggested. "But as you say, Mark, we have no evidence of that so far."

"Quite right, Chris, and I'm sure our mayor will be using that argument if he can."

After analysing the *maitre's* points in the first category they moved on.

"The second point," Mark said, "concerns infrastructure – electricity and water supply and the outflows of water and sewerage which, as we know, are usually combined into one septic tank, and what the effect of the run-off will be on the neighbouring agriculture. Louis makes very specific and important points here, because some of these issues will cost the commune or the region money if major parts of local infrastructure have to be enlarged or reinforced. But let's move on to Louis' third point, access. At the moment the château and the farm are serviced by the narrow lane which is bordered on both sides by drainage ditches and fields, except for the hundred and fifty metres with our two hedges. It's impossible for two vehicles to pass – one has to pull into a field. That rarely happens now, but what will it be like when up to one hundred guests are there for a reception, not to mention the cooks and waiters, and a band perhaps? And what about emergency access? Say someone needs an ambulance or a fire breaks out?"

"That'd be a bloody nightmare, without even starting to think about how it will affect our ability to access and leave the château," Chris said.

"Precisely. The lane will have to be significantly widened,

which means the compulsory acquisition of farmland plus digging out the water pipes and electricity cables in the ditch on our side and reinstalling them, as well as putting in new rainwater drainage. That's a huge job, and Louis says the cost would be borne by the public, not the LeBlancs."

Mark paused and took a deep breath. "It beats me how the mayor could even consider granting this authorisation. Makes me wonder if he's getting a backhander."

They worked on the draft until ten that evening and made a few amendments, agreeing that Maitre Tournier had done a first-rate job as they emailed him their go-ahead. It was now up to him to take the fight to the enemy, who in their eyes were the LeBlancs in league with the mayor, and see what happened.

8.

INTERLUDE IN LONDON

WITH pressing engagements throughout December, the family decided to celebrate Christmas in London and defer their next visit to the château to coincide with Easter in April.

On Christmas Day, Lucy was sitting next to her grandfather at lunch and told him that Yves had completed his apprenticeship with excellent references, obtained the all-important *diplome*, and was seeking a position as a *sous-chef* in a restaurant of distinction. She also said they were in love.

Since the summer Lucy had gained a junior position with an international marketing company in the West End, a job she was enjoying despite the low pay that meant she still had to live with her parents. She hoped Yves might find a job in London so they could live together, and grandfather said he would put his thinking cap on.

True to form, the OB came up trumps. His favourite dining spot was in an up-market boutique hotel in the heart of Mayfair, "My Hotel" as he called it. A few weeks after Christmas, Yves received a phone call inviting him there for an interview. Unsure what to wear, he put on a suit and tie and took along a small suitcase containing his white chef's clothing. It was a smart move.

Ernst Gaessler, a senior *sous-chef*, met him in the foyer and took him to a meeting room. Ernst had been at the hotel for ten years under the head chef, a legend in the world of gastronomy – just to work for her was an honour that gave one huge credibility. He came straight to the point.

"Why do you want to work here and what experience have you had that makes you think you are right for the job?"

Yves replied in English.

"I am in love with two things. First I am in love with *la haute cuisine*, and second with a beautiful English girl called Lucy, and I therefore seek a job in London so that I may increase my skills in the first and also be close to the second. Apart from *la diplome*" – he handed it to Ernst – "I have worked in one of the best restaurants in Toulouse, for Monsieur Michel Sarran, and also at the Auberge du Vieux Puits at Fontjoncouse for Monsieur Goujon, who have given me these references. I am sure you have heard of both these celebrated chefs."

"Yes, certainly," said Ernst, looking at the paperwork. "Now you should meet our boss, who is one of the most respected chefs in London. Why don't you slip on your work clothes and I will wait for you outside."

Within minutes Ernst was introducing Yves to a stunning French woman in her mid-forties, the celebrated queen of the kitchen known universally as "The Chef". Her hands were covered in flour, but she allowed him to "shake" her elbow.

"I know and love Sir Robert, and if Ernst thinks you're okay you have a job. I shall hope to see you soon," she said.

Yves came away with a job offer. The pay was poor, the hours appalling, *mais alors!* It was a start, and he began on February the sixteenth. Toby Burlington topped it off with a big grin by offering him a room at their place for the nights he might not be spending with Lucy.

***

Also in February, Angelique used a two-week school break to bring Mathilde to London for the assessment by Pru and her friend Nicole. They stayed with Nancy, who was indeed one of nature's grandmothers, and Mathilde took to her immediately.

In the mornings, mother and daughter went to the custom-designed music therapy centre built twenty years earlier. It was located on a single level to accommodate those in wheelchairs and had an administrative wing with an upper-floor for fundraising functions and trustee meetings.

On the ground floor there were three soundproofed rooms for therapy sessions, each with a "viewing room" separated acoustically and visually so that visitors, with the permission of the therapist, could be admitted to watch and hear a session being conducted.

As Angelique looked on keenly, Nicole and Pru introduced Mathilde to songs and simple musical activities and encouraged her to participate, aiming to improve her communication skills as well as her self-confidence. The therapists would compose songs about objects or food she was familiar with. Mathilde loved bananas, so they made up a banana song, but at some points the word "banana" was left out, encouraging her to fill in the gaps. To help her cognitive processes, they drew pictures of specific objects and asked Mathilde what they were.

They also encouraged Mathilde to join in the music by playing percussion instruments, starting with one finger and then, as she gained confidence, her hand, before progressing to a guitar. After a week she was sharing the piano stool and tentatively touching the keyboard, a clue for the therapist to build a progressive pattern of notes which could form part of a song.

Pru and Nicole also addressed her physical skills, and to exercise her muscles they encouraged her to dance to piano tunes at the end of each session.

After two weeks Mathilde was saying "Pru" and "Nic" as well as uttering words from the songs and drawings, and smiling at her mother. Angelique thought her progress was astonishing, but there was a long road ahead so she readily agreed to bring her daughter back to the centre at Easter time for more treatment.

***

Mark brought Clive Stevens, his interior designer friend, up to date on the dispute with the LeBlancs over another lunch at the Groucho Club. Clive sympathised but could offer no more advice.

"Mark, I met you in the nineties," Clive said as he tucked into his rare sirloin steak and chips, "when we built that recording studio for the company you were heading up. Solway Records, wasn't it? We talked quite a bit about what was going on in the music industry at the time. But I never knew how you happened to be where you were and, to be perfectly honest, you were a bit different to most of the people in that business. Tell me how it all started."

"I've been in the music biz since I was a teenager, Clive, when I ran bands and promoted concerts in high school with the backing of my father, who was an extremely successful businessman. When I was nineteen he told me to get a real job so I went to university, took a degree in accounting and business, and became a chartered accountant. I built up a small practice, mostly dealing with music industry people, but I couldn't stop myself from getting personally involved with some of them. I had a music publishing company and one of my first signings was a band from Australia who were chasing a record deal. Four young men all very astute musically but hopeless at business. I got them a recording contract with an independent label who respected my judgement. Their first single was a hit, they had TV and radio coverage, and I organised a national concert tour."

Mark paused to nibble a chip.

"It started well enough, in Perth, a good place because there's plenty of time to get it right before the show reaches Sydney on the other side of the continent. I signed up with a veteran promoter from the sixties who worked with every top band from the Rolling Stones onwards. His knowledge of musos' likes and dislikes was legendary. He told me about one band in his early days who used to do a forty-minute set, come off for ten, do another set, take another break, and then do a final set. A lot of energy put into a two-hour performance. At each break they'd down a Foster's and snort the coke he put in the bottle tops. Same routine every night, so he had to find a lot of beer . . . and a lot of coke. He was part of my education. Anyway, we did Adelaide and Brisbane and Melbourne, booked out, hordes of young fans on the streets trying to catch a glimpse of the band. So we hit the Sydney Entertainment Centre, which used to be the biggest arena in Australia, seated just over thirteen thousand. Our final venue. By now the band's success had begun to register overseas and record companies were phoning me for a deal."

Clive was impressed. "So you were on the verge of cracking the big time."

"That's what people were saying. For the next two years I took the band all over the English-speaking world and we got to be very close. Then the lead singer died of a heroin overdose in the dressing room after a show in London. For me that was the finish. The band kept on going with another singer – they almost didn't seem to care – but I couldn't. I still manage their songs but I'll be saying goodbye to those too when I sell the music publishing company. It's time."

"That's some roller-coaster ride. But you've survived, virtually intact as far as I can tell, and now you are going to enjoy the fruits of your labours. In France."

Mark smiled.

"Yes, Clive. Enough is definitely enough. Now finish your steak and tell me how you're doing."

***

Sir Robert's eighty-third birthday fell on the fifteenth of March, and "beware the Ides of March" was one of his favourite lines. He chose to celebrate it at "My Hotel" and invited the family and his new best friend, Alain Frugier, to join him and Lady Ann for drinks and then dinner at seven-thirty: a nice round dozen.

It had been agreed that the legal wrangle in France was off limits that evening, allowing the focus to stay firmly on "birthday boy", as the family dubbed him.

The food was amazing, *foie gras* followed by lobster and Wagyu beef ordered in advance by the OB, who had canvassed everyone's likes and dislikes. The dishes were served with special wines chosen by the sommelier. Nobody saw a menu or the prices.

"Damn the money!" the OB exclaimed. "Not too many more of these to go, I suppose, and I'm damned if I want to leave it to you lot . . . except my dearest Ann, of course."

He slipped his hand over hers as the table rippled with laughter.

"This place is some find. When did you start coming here, Robert?" asked Toby.

"Oh, must have been in the early to mid-sixties when I started to get a bit of a toehold on the advocacy ladder. Things had been pretty lean up till then, but suddenly there we were in Swinging London, the centre of the universe. Lots of lovely cases. I even got a brief for one of the people mixed up in the Profumo scandal. Do you know about that one, Alain?"

"*Mais non,* but please tell me if it will not bore your family."

"Well," said the OB, warming to his task, "this was when the so-called Establishment was really shaken up, but as always, it closed ranks and got out of a very dirty mess. In brief, the Minister for War, Jack Profumo, was having an affair with a young woman called Christine Keeler at the same time as she was alleged to be having it off with a Russian diplomat who may also have been a spy. Not good for security, you may think. Mixed up with Keeler was Stephen Ward, a London doctor and socialite who was by any standards a man who had few moral principles. He loved meeting people in high places, and one of his best entry tricks was to have lots of pretty girls around. But to get the heat off Profumo, who lied to parliament by denying his relationship with Keeler and eventually had to resign, the Establishment, led by the Home Secretary, Sir Henry Brooke, decided they needed a scapegoat, and that was Stephen Ward. He was prosecuted for living off the immoral earnings of Keeler and another girl and convicted despite the lack of evidence. That same afternoon Ward committed suicide. The Profumo affair eventually brought down the Macmillan government and . . . but what have we here?"

Sir Robert stopped and stood up as The Chef walked in. He embraced her warmly, losing the thread of the Profumo story. She was followed by Yves carrying a large cake on an even larger plate. He looked nervous but managed to set the cake down in front of Sir Robert, who was holding The Chef by the hand.

"Marvellous," he said. "This is a most unexpected surprise and I thank you."

"It is my pleasure, Robert," said The Chef. "Happy birthday. You will note that the candles spell out LXXXIII and I trust I have that correctly. There was not enough room on the cake for a candle for each year, and I know you are a scholar of Roman history, *n'est-ce pas?* Also I would like you to acknowledge my new *sous-chef* Yves, who baked this beautiful cake and whom I believe is already known to you all. As they say here: take a bow." Yves did, blushing, as they applauded.

Toby started to sing *Happy Birthday* and everyone in the dining room joined in. It was a very special moment. Then The Chef withdrew with Yves, Sir Robert blew out the candles, and stood up to personally serve a generous slice of cake to his well-wishers after calling for extra plates. He thanked everyone in the dining room for putting up with his noisy party and returned to his seat. Lady Ann spoke up after he had time to get his breath back.

"We were here once when something very bad happened. Robert, why don't you tell them about it?"

"Yes, very bad and very sad," Robert said. "Can't forget the date, November the twelfth, 1975. We were here with two very well-known friends from the music industry, Louis Benjamin and his wife, and the owner of a French record company, Leon, and his wife Elizabeth and some of his senior staff. I was representing them against another company which had used their copyrights without permission. A bit of an unusual case for me, but an interesting one. Anyway, at around nine o'clock Elizabeth went to the powder room and *BANG!* This huge noise that reminded some of us of The Blitz. She came running back in, crying out that there was a huge explosion. "Yes, Elizabeth, we heard you", Louis said. A crass remark I suppose, but it broke the tension and everyone relaxed. I remember the famous bandleader Joe Loss was at the next table with a big party and they all laughed too.

"But it wasn't funny because the IRA had tossed a shrapnel bomb into Scott's Oyster Bar next door which killed one person and seriously injured several others. Just one of many acts of terrorism from that era. We were ushered out by heavily armed police around an hour later. Won't forget that night."

Sir Robert regaled his guests with more tales over dessert and coffee. When Yves returned, dressed for going out, he was given a glass of wine and became, with Lucy, the centre of attention. Then the party broke up after a final toast to the Old Bastard, who ordered them all to be there again at the same time next year when he'd blow out some more candles.

***

Maitre Tournier had received his copy of the submission made by the *avocats* appointed by the *conseil municipal* on behalf of the mayor, and the one lodged by the LeBlancs.

The mayor attempted to argue that Tournier's submission went in too late, but this was easily scotched because Tournier had photographic as well as verbal evidence of the date the authorisation was made public. The mayor also tried to prove that he had received approvals from instrumentalities including the Department of Agriculture, but these authorisations predated the purchase of the farm by the LeBlancs and did not refer to the specific nature nor size of the works to be carried out. Furthermore, any proposed changes to infrastructure had been adjudicated as matters to be negotiated with the various authorities *after* the tribunal gave its planning permission.

The submission on behalf of the LeBlanc family followed the same line as the mayor's, as well as making a snide insinuation that the English owners of the château were unworthy foreigners who came and went as they pleased to enjoy the French countryside but weren't prepared to put up with any inconveniences. Pru recalled the article in *La Depeche* about *midges*, but Maitre Tournier implied that he could demolish that *canard* with ease.

"Still," Tournier said during one discussion on the telephone, "you must understand, Mark, that the tribunal consists of two judges, both of whom are steeped in our law and practice but are still human, with the emotions and prejudices we all share. In this case I feel that we have an eighty per cent chance of success, but I have to tell you that I have won cases I did not expect to win and lost a few which I was almost certain to win. Now we have to be patient. This issue may come before the tribunal in just weeks, but it's more likely that it will be months before we are given a result. Meanwhile, enjoy your beautiful home in France and I will do all I can to help you."

***

Toby was in his office on Canary Wharf, trying to use his laptop and iPhone while eating a chicken and pesto bagel delivered by Hungryhouse. He was not happy.

"How's lithium doing now?" Andrew McAllister, the bank's recently hired clean energy expert, called out from his desk.

"It's in fucking free fall," Toby snarled as he tracked the share price updates on his computer screen. "I don't get it. For months it's been on the up – a few minor blips, but always up – until this. There's nothing to show why. It's gotta be some huge player out there who's selling short. We don't know who it is or why they're doing it. Can't be just speculation, there must be something driving it."

"Well there's a bit of an upsurge here in solar, and Jim told me the other energy stocks are all doing okay. Have you looked at the main lithium users?"

"Yes. As we know they're nearly all in the electric car market and Tesla's the front runner. But forget lithium, what really concerns me is the fact that a huge proportion of the stock exchange value is tied up in the social media sector and Amazon and outfits who have no saleable assets. Some aren't even making a profit."

"But they're today's new industries. They're way past the start-up stage. Take Amazon. On its current market value Jeff Bezos is the richest man in the world."

"That's my point, Andrew. All Amazon owns is some inventory, and probably not that much. Most of the things they sell come from other suppliers. They're totally dependent on their electronic networks. And should something go wrong and the personal data of all their customers is suddenly spread worldwide, or say the Chinese or Russians want to cause havoc by hacking in and disrupting their business, it could be all over, red rover."

Toby took another bite of his bagel. "Google and YouTube are even more vulnerable. And what about Apple? Sure, it has real products, but it depends on the revenue from its apps and all its advertising. One of Apple's major threats is coming from Spotify. They're looking to make a huge private offering if the rumours are right. What does Spotify have? Absolutely zip except agreements to stream other people's music."

"So?"

"That's where to look for tomorrow's great crash, Andrew."

Toby finished his bagel and went out for a walk to clear his head. His longer-term algorithms were all pointing south, but he couldn't figure out what was going to be the trigger.

9.

ADILAH'S SAD STORY

THE Easter holidays were approaching and the weather forecast for the south-west of France promised warm and sunny days. It was agreed that Mark would go to the château in advance of Pru and the Burlingtons to open it up and see the gardeners, before meeting Maitre Tournier. He was also determined to have a rendezvous with the mayor and express his outrage at the recent turn of events.

Mark could almost feel the grand old building stretching itself as he went around unlocking the shutters and windows, after being closed off from the outside world through the long months of winter. Bernard and Francois walked in from the garden, happy to see him and saying said how angry they were on hearing about the LeBlanc family's plans.

"Monsieur LeBlanc was here last week with a man I did not like the look of," Bernard said. "He asked me to look after the garden when his family moved into the farmhouse, but I said I would never go near it. I should tell you though, Mark, that quite a few people in this and the neighbouring communes are in favour of their development because it may provide work. Firstly for the local artisans like the family Delpas who are builders, and later on for people who are prepared to do part-time jobs as cooks and waiters and cleaners. There are not too many opportunities for work around here."

Mark saw Bernard's point and nodded. Then they discussed the busy spring schedule for the garden and the park and Mark departed to see Louis Tournier, after first keeping another appointment he had made. He dropped in to see Tomas at the estate agent's office in Toulouse and was greeted warmly.

"I have heard that your new neighbours have received permission for some major developments but I do not know the details," Tomas said. "Could you tell me, please?"

Mark explained the authorisation approvals and repeated what he had told Tomas on the phone.

"What I now seek, Tomas, are your views on the saleability and potential effect on the value of the château if this goes ahead."

Tomas thought it over before replying.

"Monsieur Escott. I know that you would like to be reassured in this matter, but you should know the truth. At this moment, with the tribunal still pending, neither the château nor the farm could be sold. Who would want to buy with such a huge decision outstanding? After a decision is handed down we should consider what sort of buyer we could be looking for. Typically, the château would appeal to a wealthy, probably self-made Parisian. Most Parisians with, as you say 'old money', already have family estates. Or alternatively, maybe a person from another country, English, German or Dutch most likely. But the château will only be attractive to such a buyer – perhaps a family like yours – if it can be enjoyed in peace, which means that you must win at the tribunal. If you lose, I fear the château will be difficult to sell at any price, and certainly one that is probably only half of your current investment."

Mark was gobsmacked. "Jesus, Tomas. You're saying we could lose hundreds of thousands?"

"That is an unfortunate possibility, Monsieur Escott. But there is one other thing that occurs to me. If the family LeBlanc are successful and permission is granted to expand into a commercial enterprise, it might be possible that the owners of the château could also consider applying for the rights to turn it into a commercial establishment as well. A hotel or a resort perhaps? It is difficult to see how permission could be refused. That is not an option for you, I am sure, but it could appeal to someone else. It is just a thought."

Mark began to mull over Tomas's opinion, and after further discussion he thanked him and headed off to see Louis.

Down the sunny boulevards of Toulouse he noticed that the women were already wearing colourful and fashionable summer dresses. Spring has really arrived here, he thought, comparing it with the dour weather back in London, and feeling that whatever was to happen with the château, buying this little piece of France had been a good family decision.

As Louis had nothing new to report, Mark was soon on his way back to Saint Audan.

Early the next morning Mark rang the mayor at home.

"I would like to see you, Michel, so we can talk about recent events and why you have not been in contact with us."

"Certainement," Michel replied, sounding as if he had been expecting the call. "I have a meeting this afternoon but I should be home by eighteen hundred hours, and if I am late Adilah can entertain you."

On arriving at six o'clock Mark noticed that the mayor's car wasn't there. He rang the front door bell and Adilah beckoned him inside. She was wearing a loose, rose-coloured silk peignoir, and as soon as she closed the door she clasped Mark tightly to her. It was evident that she wasn't wearing anything else. Her lips moved over his as she rolled her tongue into his mouth.

"Hold me, touch me," she begged, wrapping her arms around his back and moving her body against his.

For the briefest of moments Mark was tempted, until he remembered all those times in his earlier days as a rock 'n' roll manager when young would-be stars would throw themselves at him – and all those times he didn't resist. He gently pushed Adilah away and her robe parted for him to behold the shape of a goddess.

"Stop. We cannot do this," he said.

Adilah stepped back, covered herself, and looked at Mark, seeing concern but no lust. She burst into tears.

"He will kill me," she sobbed.

Mark could not help feeling sorry for this gorgeous and emotional woman. He put his arm round her shoulders and drew her to the bottom of the stairs.

"Go and put some other clothes on and I will wait for you here, Adilah," he said.

"If you stay I will tell you my sad story," she said, drying her eyes.

"I'll be here," he repeated.

Five minutes later Adilah came back down the stairs, wearing a floral dress and fresh makeup. She led Mark into the sitting room and they sat together on a deep leather couch.

"Adilah, you said 'he will kill me'. What do you mean?"

She tenderly placed a hand on his forearm and took a deep breath.

"I will try to explain. This is my sad story. It starts just over forty years ago in Morocco. You have heard of Casablanca perhaps? It is the largest city in the country and one of the most important ports in the whole of North Africa. Well, my mother was a *putain* there, a whore. She never told me who my father was – it's possible she did not know. But she talked to me about love and how it was best to avoid it, so I always felt that maybe in an earlier life she had enjoyed a romantic affair which had gone wrong. As a whore she gave herself to whoever could pay, and because she was still quite young and pretty there were many, mostly seamen. We lived in a small apartment in a house that contained several whores, and the rule was that if you were busy you hung a cross on your front door.

"For my first few years I was always put in the back room when my mother was, how do you say, 'entertaining'. But when I was five she insisted I attend school, and with that and lessons on Islam at the mosque I was rarely at home in the daytime, when she mostly had her clients. She paid a minder – a great brute of a fellow he was – to send new clients to her, but also to let them know that he would severely harm them if they did not behave properly. Most of the time that worked. But Islam is a religion that allows men to dominate women, so those like my mother do not have an easy time. And prostitution is illegal, so they are even more vulnerable."

Mark wanted to say something, but he couldn't find the right words to interrupt her tragic, unfolding story.

"And then came AIDS. As in most of the world, Moroccans did not for some time know what it was or how it was spread. Men would not think of wearing a condom and contraception was left up to the woman, so prostitutes were highly vulnerable and it spread right through them. My mother became ill in the mid-nineteen eighties and died very quickly. It was terrible to watch and know that there was no cure for her. As for me . . . well, I suppose I was lucky. When I told the people at the mosque, they took me to a home for young orphans. In those days adoption was virtually illegal and rarely practiced, except for some children whose parents were both known members of the Islamic faith. Children just roamed the streets. But I soon discovered that this so-called shelter was really, as I think you say, a cover for terrible things. Once the boys turned thirteen they were given – more like sold – to the owners of factories, or sent off to work on merchant ships. It was like slave labour. And the girls, once they reached puberty they were offered to men seeking a young bride. They were condemned to a life of rape and treated like dogs."

She paused, and Mark thought of his own youth when, as an articled clerk, he had done the audit of the Southwark Catholic Rescue Society which sheltered and put out for adoption unwanted children, thus providing the faith with new recruits and, he had always imagined, a ready-made pool of young Catholic women available for marriage – in return perhaps for a nice donation. Different faith, same business model.

As they drank from the glasses of wine she had poured earlier, Adilah began to cut to the chase.

"I was fourteen when Michel came into my life. He was twenty years older than me and good-looking and friendly, and at least to start with quite loving. Between the shelter and Michel they obtained a new birth certificate which made me eligible for marriage and a passport, and I escaped from Morocco. Suddenly I was in France! Michel was in business then as a motor mechanic, but he knew that he would one day inherit his father's farm, so we lived close by in the little cottage just down the lane. We had two children – a girl and a boy – and for a time I think we were both quite happy. But sadly that came to an end."

"Do you really want to tell me all this?" asked Mark.

"Yes, I want to and I need to. Mark, I really like you and in different times I could love you. Not like earlier tonight but really, and so I can tell you things that I have never told anyone else. May I go on?"

He nodded.

"You know Christian de Montfort? Yes, well, as you say 'out of the blue', Michel told me that I was to become his mistress and it was not up to me to agree or not. It was already agreed. And I had to obey."

"*What?*" Mark exclaimed in disbelief. "How could he do that?"

"There is something that Christian holds over Michel, but I know not what it is. This was not easy, as Christian is not a nice man. He treated me like a whore, like my mother, all he was interested in was my body. But after two years he got bored with me because I refused to talk to him. However, that was not the end of it. Since then Michel has ordered me to have sex with other men. You are the latest."

"What is going on, Adilah? And why me?" Mark asked.

"Honestly, I do not know. These days Michel is only interested in two things, money and power. When he inherited his father's estate the farm and some money came to him, but not enough to live in comfort. So I think he has done some deals over property developments for which he has received a small brown envelope. I know he has a bank account in Switzerland, and I think he uses it to hide away the contents of those envelopes. Eleven years ago he was elected to our *conseil municipal* and seven years ago he became the mayor. It can be difficult to find someone willing to take on that position in a small commune like ours, but Michel saw it as a way to exercise power – mayors have a surprising amount of it – and make money too. You know all those new houses in the commune, including the eight on our own land? Well, they were all built with authorisations handed out by Michel, and most of them are on small parcels of land owned by farmers or their children who are not well off, so many in the community are not unhappy with him in the least."

"Well I can see why he might have given that authorisation to the LeBlancs, but I am still at a loss to understand why he wants you to seduce me."

"It is a mystery to me also, but for some reason which I do not know he is frightened of you, Mark."

"Frightened of me? Why? I'm no threat to him."

"I am sure of it. There is something about your actions in trying to overturn the planning permission for LeBlanc which makes Michel very nervous. If I seduced you it would give him power over you, because you are a married man and would want to keep it secret. Now that I have failed to do his wishes he will be even more worried about you and angry with me."

"Does he mistreat you?"

"Usually not physically, although sometimes he has hit me. More often he uses the children against me. He tells them I am nothing more than a whore like my mother, and he tells Louisa that it's genetic and she will end up the same."

"That's appalling. What in the—." He stopped as they heard a car pulling up.

"Now you have heard my sad story, or most of it," Adilah said.

Mark just had time to say "Call me any time if you need help" when the front door opened and Michel walked in.

"Please accept my apologies, and I hope Adilah has been looking after you," said the mayor, shaking hands with Mark and turning to his wife. "*Ma chere*, please open a fresh bottle of wine and pour me a glass so that I may speak with our friend who has been so patient to wait for me."

He looked enquiringly at Mark and they sat down while Adilah did as requested and left the room.

"So, my friend, you wish to speak to me about the planning authorisation the commune has granted to Monsieur and Madame LeBlanc. But let me first say a few things. Since I have been mayor, seven years now, I have seen as my main task the repopulation of our commune. For several decades our numbers declined and we could no longer support even a small shop. Now the village school is in danger of being closed as there are fewer children. In France we call this *desertification*."

"Excuse me," Mark interrupted, "but you cannot possibly expect or even want to turn this commune back into what it was like a hundred years ago. The land does not need so many people to work it with so much mechanisation and the aggregation of so many small landholdings into bigger farms. You know as well as I do that even in the last fifty years the proportion of the population employed on the land has fallen from fifteen per cent to three per cent. And as for this commune, the population has actually doubled from two hundred and sixty to five hundred and thirty since 1990. You gave me those figures yourself. Remember?"

The mayor looked put out by the vehemence of Mark's interjection but continued.

"Yes, I agree with your figures. However, you must understand that many of the younger people we have attracted to live here would welcome the possibility of a local job, even if it was only part-time or occasional. If they have young children it also helps them to meet similar people in the commune."

Mark changed tack.

"Whatever. As you know, Michel, my family has lodged an appeal with the tribunal and we shall vigorously oppose any attempt by the LeBlancs to go through with their plan. We understand this process may take years and cost all three parties a lot of money. Do the rest of the *conseil municipal* have these facts and know how much this might cost the community? Did they know the extent of the works you authorised and did they agree? I think not, although I shall find out. But the thing that upsets me the most is your attempt to push this matter through without our knowledge, when only a few months ago you were telling me not to worry in the slightest about anything. That seems very deceitful."

Mark had had enough of trying to express himself accurately in French. "Monsieur le Maire, I have to leave. But this is not the end of the conversation." He stormed out without shaking hands or saying goodbye to Adilah.

Later, alone except for a large glass of Dewar's scotch on the rocks, Mark went over Adilah's story. He believed it but thought she was a good actress, and although he liked her he knew he had to be careful. As for the mayor, he regarded him with contempt. There was only one possible reason for Ricard's failure to inform him of the LeBlanc application: it would make him miss the deadline for an appeal. He thought it either indicated that Ricard himself had doubts about the grounds for granting the authorisation – or there was something very fishy going on behind the scenes.

10.

FRIENDS AND FOES

MARK didn't have to wait long to find out. Next morning he received an unexpected visit from the farmer who owned most of the land adjacent to the château and the farm, Monsieur Lestrade.

"Monsieur Escott, I have been away and just heard that these *salauds* – bastards – the LeBlancs want to turn this commune into a cheap party venue," he exploded. "Our lanes will be clogged with young men driving too fast and constantly using their horns. As for us farmers, who cares if we cannot plough our fields or reap our crops because our noise would spoil the enjoyment of these party people who do not even live here. Bah! I have just seen LeBlanc and told him what I think, and do you know what he said? 'It is old *vieilles badernes* – old fogeys – like you who stop France making progress into the modern world.' Well I'll make him think again! One of my tractors is about to break down in the lane and the mechanic won't be able to move it until tomorrow."

Mark could not suppress a smile. He knew Lestrade because he mowed their fields and accepted the hay from the northern paddock in recompense. But he was a fiery customer.

"Do you think the other farmers in the commune share your views, Monsieur Lestrade?" he asked.

"The older ones will. The younger ones maybe not. I will find out at our next meeting, which will be in late April. I will also ask the man from the Department of Agriculture what in God's name were they thinking when they did not object to this application. We must fight these dirty foreigners coming into our region and turning it into a wasteland."

Mark smiled again at the use of the word "foreigners".

"It is so encouraging for me to hear you say this, and speaking to the department is an excellent idea, Monsieur Lestrade. Perhaps you can tell me what they say. I am asking for a formal meeting with the mayor and his deputies tomorrow and I will advise you of the outcome."

Lestrade agreed and left, still fulminating at the *sales étrangers*.

"One down and lots to go," Mark said to himself while opening the local telephone book. He wanted to speak to every member of the *conseil municipal* individually, as well as the other landowners in the commune, and jotted down their numbers.

***

Mark arrived at the *Mairie* at two o'clock the next afternoon for a meeting with Ricard and the two deputy mayors he met at the *apero* a year ago, Lionel Cros, the farmer, and Julien Deschamps, the electrician.

Ricard began by saying this was an informal meeting held at the request of Monsieur Escott and no minutes would be taken. Then he ran through the procedures he had followed, the government departments he had contacted, and the advice he had received before making his decision on the LeBlanc matter. At this point Deschamps remarked that at the meeting where the mayor advised him and his fellow councillors of the application, seeking their approval for rubber-stamping it, he had no idea of the size or scope of the planned enlargement, and asked if he could now see all the documentation. Mark obliged and the deputies examined it.

Ten minutes later Julien Deschamps spoke up.

"With due respect, Monsieur le Maire, had you shown us this documentation at the meeting there would have been much discussion. Whilst we understand that the decision is solely yours, I would have appreciated being more fully informed. Now we have no choice but to support that decision and await the outcome of the tribunal."

"I agree with my colleague," Lionel Cros said. "And I would add that I am amazed that the Department of Agriculture, for which I am our commune's spokesperson, gave a favourable opinion to this application. I request that copies of the submissions by all three parties, Messieurs Escott and LeBlanc and the commune, be made available to us so that we can see the arguments being put forward. I also ask what potential costs might be incurred by the commune should the tribunal decide against us."

The mayor looked miffed, but he agreed to produce the documentation and the cost estimates

Mark was given permission to speak.

"Gentlemen, I thank you for giving up your valuable time for this meeting, and for your opinions, Monsieur Cros and Monsieur Deschamps. While I respect your support of our mayor, I should tell you that my brother-in-law and I intend to fight this authorisation all the way, and we have been told that the decision of the tribunal is open to higher courts of law, including the European courts. We have invested a large sum of money in the château, but fortunately we have adequate funds for a long struggle. I am sorry that this may become a heavy burden on the finances of the commune, of which we too are a part. But this decision was reached without any discussion with us, and we at the château are the ones most directly affected. I bid you all *au revoir* and thank you again."

And so the battle lines were drawn.

Over the ensuing weeks Mark contacted the councillors and most of the major landowners in the commune, and his suspicions were confirmed. There were some local people for the proposal and some against. One councillor, Marie-Anne Delpas, put her view very clearly.

"Monsieur Escott, I have sympathy for the views of you and your family, but for us younger people it may prove to be a great opportunity. Some of us have children and our husbands must travel to major centres like Toulouse to find employment. That means leaving home early and getting home late, with no chance of taking the children to school or picking them up. That is left to us, the mothers. But if there was more local employment, even part-time, we could earn some money and also enjoy some social interaction. I was brought up here and I love it, which is why I volunteered to be on the *conseil*, but very few of us work on the land and we have skills that we are not using. I for instance worked as the personal assistant to a marketing director before I had our first child."

Mark had to respect her views, and said so. He also had to give some thought about how to get the local population on side.

***

Later that month Lionel Cros asked Mark if he could have an

hors du record meeting, off the record, at which he was brief and to the point.

"I saw the Department of Agriculture today about a number of other matters and I was talking to a senior man I know very well," Cros said. "I told him about your problem. He was astounded and said the department would not have approved the application if they had been told the full extent of the project. This land is zoned for agriculture, and what is being proposed is clearly a total change of usage. I have looked at all the correspondence the mayor has given us and I cannot find anything that defines the works which are proposed. There are letters to and from the department, but they were written well before the LeBlanc family even arrived here, and this is most unusual. It is almost as if the mayor was looking at some lesser development and has used the department's positive responses to justify his approval for this application by the LeBlancs. That is quite wrong. But, Mark, it is not Lionel Cros who has told you this."

Mark thanked Lionel and promptly telephoned Maitre Tournier. After listening to Mark, his *avocat* said, "That could explain several things which were not clear. However, the problem now is that the final date for submissions to the tribunal is long passed. All I can do when the date and composition of the tribunal is announced is try to inform the members of our suspicions. From time to time I can find an open ear."

By this time Toby and Jenny had arrived at the château and the days were lengthening. The plane trees in the park were showing their first signs of greenery, and the tulips that Mark and Bernard planted in autumn were nodding their multi-coloured heads in the gentle westerly breeze.

Alain Frugier called to say he was heading back to London

from a conference in Bordeaux, so he was invited for lunch on the way. After being brought up to speed on the battle lines Alain offered his thoughts.

"Several things are very interesting," he said. "Firstly, the LeBlancs are not a wealthy family, therefore they must be borrowing the money to buy and then renovate and expand the farm. As Toby pointed out, they would need at least one and a half million euros to do all this. Where does the money to cover the mortgage come from? They would require a big income from hiring out a reception centre and catering services every weekend, year in and year out, and I cannot imagine that is remotely possible in an area like this. The figures do not add up."

"Exactly my point, Alain," Toby chimed in. "So what is their plan?"

"Think laterally, *mes amis*. What is the other effect of this authorisation? In the words of your estate agent it has made this house, your lovely château, almost unsaleable – except perhaps to someone who wants to buy it at a very cheap price. Who might that be?"

"You French," said Jenny. "You have minds like rubber bands. You can twist them around anything. I never thought of that, but it does make sense."

"Please correct me if I'm misunderstanding you, Alain," said Pru. "You think that perhaps there is a sly strategy behind the LeBlancs' purchase and planning application? To enable them, or someone else, to buy the château cheaply and then sell it, and perhaps the farm too, for a nice tidy profit? And ditch the planning permission, even if it is authorised by the tribunal?"

"Well, that is certainly one scenario," Alain allowed, "although the market conditions for properties in this part of France would not be encouraging at the moment. But maybe there is another one. Perhaps they have some even bigger plans for developing the château and the farm, and the current planning permission before the tribunal is just testing the water."

"And you French think we British are devious!" Jenny exclaimed.

***

It was time for a break from worrying about the château to enjoy the company of friends and family. Pru and Jenny, after consulting their husbands, had invited their mother and father, their children and grandchildren, and two other couples, all longstanding acquaintances.

They began arriving for a week on Sunday the nineteenth of June, 2016, and everyone was looking forward to a break in the unremitting media deluge on the Europe referendum known universally as "Brexit".

It was a full house and Alice was kept busy twelve hours a day, preparing the guest rooms and working on the menus. The two sisters decided on an evening to celebrate French gastronomy and prepared a special menu that included an appetiser of *foie gras* followed by *escargots*, or *crevettes* for those who didn't like snails. There was a main course of local wild boar, *daube de sanglier*, marinated for twenty-four hours in onions, garlic, cloves, carrots, thyme, orange peel and red wine, and then cooked for three and half hours before a cup of cognac was added for thirty minutes. Anybody who didn't like this was expected to put on a brave face while eating it.

After some banter at pre-dinner drinks the main course was consumed in silence, and the younger ones waited patiently for the OB to finish, replenishing their glasses with the excellent Gevrey-Chambertin provided by the two visiting couples.

Alice and Lucy cleared the table and brought in an aficionado's assortment of gourmet cheeses, traditional varieties as well as goat cheese and sheep milk *fromage*. Most of the guests were too full to nibble more than a small selection – and they knew that a dessert of *crème brulée* was to follow.

As the coffee arrived, Toby produced an A4 notebook and took a ballpoint pen from his pocket.

"Right, ladies and gentlemen," he proclaimed. "I propose that we each put in ten pounds – not euros – and hazard a guess at the result of tomorrow's referendum. The guess will be made in terms of the percentage difference between the Remain vote and the Leave vote, and the person nearest the final result will scoop the pool. May I have your opinions please, starting with my brother-in-law who has always been good with a decimal point or even two."

Mark said, "Well clearly I'm expecting a comfortable win for David Cameron and Remain. I know this is in line with virtually all the opinion polls, but I'm not going to be too adventurous. So I'll put the margin at three per cent, 51.5 versus 48.5."

"Not for the first time I'm agreeing with my husband," said Pru. "But I cannot believe the great British public will do less than vote resoundingly for Remain. They are not stupid, and when you look at the people backing the campaign for an exit – yuck! I'm going 55 per cent for Remain and 45 for Leave."

The Old Bastard interjected. "Do I hear my elder daughter calling me stupid? Mister chairman, I would ask that you insist on contestants moderating their language. I am of the firm belief that the great British public is heartily sick of the European Union and especially its politicians and bureaucrats. Their interference in British affairs, their over-riding of British laws, of which I am particularly aware, and the enormous costs involved – which fall back on the British taxpayer – have long convinced me that we should never have joined the EU in the first place and now we have a chance of leaving. Take it, I say, and I believe the polls have got it wrong, which they are in the habit of doing lately. The result will be 52 for Leave and 48 for Remain. And I believe my wife – your mother, Prudence – will support my view and share my winnings."

Lady Ann nodded and added, "Aye aye, sir."

Most opinions around the table supported Mark and Pru, although several people had reservations, particularly about the EU's uncompromising stance on the free movement of people as well as goods and finances. Lucy was one of them.

"Yves is French and he has the right to work in England," she said. "London needs people coming in, but that may not be the case for Bradford or other places in the north, which already have high unemployment."

Robin Bromley, one of the new guests, took up her point and offered a different view from someone on the frontline.

"I'm a doctor, as you know, and I run one of the major surgical units at the Royal Marsden Hospital in the Fulham Road. We can be called upon to provide emergency surgery at any time of the day or night, seven days a week. We have a very big team of surgeons, anaesthetists and nurses, not to mention cleaning staff. I couldn't run the place if I couldn't employ nurses from Asia, mostly Indonesians and Filipinos, and probably ninety per cent of the cleaners are from Eastern Europe. If we leave Europe and a future government starts putting in quotas on immigrants we won't be able to keep going. British women don't want those jobs with low pay and bad hours, and who can blame them? Plus there's the prohibitive costs of living in or commuting to central London. I can only hope that the result is Remain and I'll go for a four-point margin, 52 to 48."

Apart from the OB's strong objections to the sway the

European Union had over the United Kingdom, the chief argument for Leave seemed to be the fear that unfettered immigration would take jobs away from British workers, but nobody could be specific about where and in what industries that might happen. As Chris put it: "I was talking to a young colleague the other day. He lives in a small town in Sussex and said he was worried about migrants. Surely not in Hassocks, I said. Do you have *any* immigrants. 'No,' he said, 'we don't, but it's not Hassocks I'm worried about'."

At last it was Toby's turn.

"I would just like to say a few general words about the government and tomorrow's vote," he said. "To begin with, Cameron didn't need to promise a referendum and he should know that public opinion can be very fickle. He got back in this time, mostly, I reckon, because would-be Lib-Dem supporters like me were pissed off with Nick Clegg playing footsie with Cameron, and because Labour were unable to come up with some viable alternative strategies to the Conservatives' austerity programs. We all know they are hurting the poor a damn sight more than they're hurting the rich. But the public may – just may – give Cameron a kick up the arse tomorrow, and my forecast is for a win for Leave by 51 to 49."

The late sun was fading and so were the visitors, most of whom called it a night as they were leaving early in the morning after their week at the château. Lady Ann and the OB said good evening, and Mark suggested a nightcap to his brother-in-law.

"You just could be right about the vote," Mark said. "But you wouldn't personally want that, would you? You make heaps from your gig with the bank and lots more on the side. That could all get a bit dodgy if some of the finance houses move shop out of London to Frankfurt or Paris."

"To tell you the truth, Mark, I'm disgusted with the way

Cameron and the Tories have handled – or mishandled – the whole aftermath of the GFC," Toby said. "The banks and the other lenders are no more regulated now than they were in 2008. My algorithms are all telling me we're heading for a crash that will make the last one look like a blip, and if I'm right there won't be any talk about a bank or anyone else being too big to fail. Just read the signs. They're all there, but nobody in my business wants to see them because we're all making pots of money. You've got money in shares and pension funds, like I do, but if ever I tell you to *SELL*, then believe me. Do it, and do it bloody fast."

On that warning note, Toby and Mark followed the others indoors, locked up and went to bed.

11.

UNEXPECTED NEWS

THE news first broke at the other end of the world, in *The Sydney Morning Herald*: "There have been social media reports that a major international hotel group based in Sydney is looking to expand its activities into Europe."

Reporter Don Brenner interviewed Tom Watson, managing director and CEO of the Frontline Hotel Group, to confirm that it was looking at acquiring a substantial property with a view to establishing a luxury resort in the south-west of France.

"Things are at a very early stage, but yes we are. This sort of resort would cater for international businessmen seeking a place to relax that provided access to the very latest in communication technology," Watson was quoted as saying. "For instance, it would provide online access to interpreters of all languages, and also maintain a small fleet of helicopters to take clients to the main business hubs of Bordeaux, Toulouse and Marseilles less than an hour away."

The report went on to say that while Watson had some properties in mind, the region was predominantly agricultural, and getting planning approval for a zoning change would be no easy matter in France. However, he claimed there could be a precedent: an application to turn a château in the village of Saint Audan into a resort was about to be lodged by its British owners. Watson confirmed that this project was in line with the visionary expansion plans of Frontline, which was owned by a consortium of Chinese property developers and operated resorts near Sydney, Melbourne and Perth.

The mayor rang Mark. He was clearly agitated.

"Adilah just saw on Facebook that a big developer is planning to build a luxury resort here," Michel said. "One of her friends was surprised when she saw the mention of Saint Audan and copied it to her. Can it possibly be true?"

"A friend of mine in Australia just sent it to me too," Mark said casually. "I know the fellow who represents the developers, Tom Watson, and we stay in touch. I've mentioned our situation to him and we both think this is a great investment opportunity. If it all went ahead you'd have a thriving business community right here in Saint Audan, wouldn't you? First the LeBlancs' new reception centre and then a flash resort, creating plenty of jobs. Just what you've been looking for, Michel."

There was silence at the other end of the line.

"I am not sure that this is what everybody wants. I shall have to think. *Au revoir.*"

News of the resort proposal spread through the commune like wildfire. Soon friends were turning into foes and foes were becoming friends. Tweets were flying around and the major newspaper serving the south-west picked up the story the next day.

Mark called a family meeting and flew to London with Pru, taking a suite at the hotel where Yves worked so they could talk in confidence over dinner.

Sir Robert and Lady Ann were the first to arrive.

"By Jove," said the OB to Mark as he grabbed a scotch,

"you've set some hares running in your time, my boy, but this one is the biggest yet. Knowing you a bit over the last thirty-odd years, I'd say you might have something up your sleeve. I'll wait till you tell us, but here's looking at you."

He raised his glass to Mark, who smiled and returned the salute. "May have learned a few things from you over that time, you old bastard."

Christopher came straight from chambers and was next to arrive.

"Sorry, but Diane won't be able to make it," he said. "Sends her apologies but she couldn't get the usual babysitter and the kids are hard work for a new one."

He joined his grandmother on the settee and clinked his gin and tonic with her glass of dry sherry.

After giving her fiancé a hug and a kiss, to the applause and cat-calls of the other kitchen staff, Lucy came up to the suite.

"Thanks for inviting me, and Yves sends his love and best wishes," she said as Mark gave her a glass of wine.

Toby and Jenny were the last to arrive.

"Don't know whether to buy or sell," Toby quipped to Mark. "You've certainly buggered all my algorithms this time."

"Okay," Mark said. "Let's order dinner for eight o'clock. That'll give us an hour for talking."

With that done and everyone's glass refilled, Mark began.

"Sorry, Toby, but I'm going back to my old mantra: what do we want and how do we get it. Or in planning-speak—'

"First objectives, secondly strategies, and then tactics," Toby interrupted.

"Damned if you haven't actually learned something, Toby," Mark said. "Let's start by redefining our objectives. Would everyone agree that our principal objective is to safeguard the château and our hopes for a tranquil life there in our retirement years, and ensure its continuing value as a major investment?"

There was a murmur of agreement.

"Right. And so far we have done all we can to defend that tranquillity against the threat of the LeBlancs' development plans. Until the tribunal hands down a decision there's not a lot more we can do. But another scenario has been suggested to us by our friend, Alain Frugier. He thinks that perhaps the LeBlanc threat is a smokescreen designed to drive down the resale value of the château, which it already has, and allow an unknown party to come in and steal it. At first I could hardly give any credibility to this idea, but think about it. We turn up, buy a run-down château, spend a bomb on the renovations and turn it into a showpiece – and now someone could waltz in and buy it for a song. Alain's theory might be far-fetched, but I thought we should test it out."

"So, by Jove, somehow you've got these Chinese developers interested in our little château. How'd you do that?" asked the OB.

"Or is it just *The Sydney Morning Herald* that thinks you have?" Lucy asked.

"Go to the top of the class, Lucy," Mark replied. "We've all heard politicians and others complaining about fake news, but now this isn't just a rumour on Twitter, it's a fact supported by a reputable Australian newspaper as well as the media in south-west France. Amazing what can happen when an old mate plants a juicy seed in the right place."

Toby proposed a toast to Tom Watson and they raised their glasses.

"I heard Michel Ricard being interviewed on radio just before I left," Mark continued. "He couldn't add much to the story except to say that he had spoken to me and I didn't deny it. You could tell he was rattled and really pissed off."

It was Chris's turn to have a say.

"Dad, only a few years ago I had to show you how to switch on your iPhone. Now you're a bloody media manipulator. Not sure whether to be proud of you or have you put somewhere where you can't get yourself into trouble."

"Mark, I'm just glad you're not running a hedge fund or you'd put the rest of us out of business," Toby added.

The OB was confounded, but congratulated Mark again for putting the cat among the pigeons.

Mark went on.

"My feeling is that the story will be a one-day wonder except in our little neck of the woods, which is where we want it to simmer. We're not going to deny it. If anyone asks, we just smile and say *peut-etre*. We sit back and see if anything happens, and if it doesn't, we haven't lost anything."

They all agreed and went on their way after dinner.

However, something did happen almost as soon as Mark and Pru returned to France. A man purporting to be a real estate agent called them.

"Monsieur Escott?" he said. "I am calling from Toulouse where I represent the interests of some prominent businessmen. We understand you are selling the Château du Moulin."

"Well, it's possible."

"Then may I come to talk with you?"

"Of course, but please understand that nothing has been decided."

"I will come tomorrow if you are available. Say ten-thirty?"

"That's fine. I shall see you then."

Next morning a new-model Citroen stopped at the front door of the château and a shortish man in an expensive suit got out to meet Mark and Pru.

"*Bonjour*, Monsieur Escott. I have the pleasure to introduce

121

myself: Nicolas Demey."

"*Bonjour*, Monsieur Demey, and please call me Mark. May I introduce you to my wife, Prudence."

"The pleasure is mine," Demey said, smiling at Pru as they ushered him indoors.

"Would you like to look around?" Pru asked.

"You are most kind, Madame, but I have received a briefing from my client who has a good idea of what you have here, and may I say it is absolutely *magnifique* – or as I believe one might say in English, stunning."

They walked through the hall, where a dark-timbered Bechstein grand piano had recently been installed, to the sitting room. Demey accepted an expresso coffee as Mark pointed him to a lounge chair.

"*Merci*," he said, declining the sugar bowl. "Madame Prudence and Monsieur Mark, I will come quickly to the point. We have heard and read that, for whatever your reasons, you are considering the sale of this excellent property to some Asian developers. Now we, and I speak for both my client and myself, have nothing against Asian people. Come to Toulouse and you will see hundreds from many different countries. But these old châteaux are part of our French heritage and we do not want to see this one turned into what the media are calling a luxury resort. However, if you are in fact looking to sell, my client might be interested, depending on the price of course."

"Really?" said Mark, feigning surprise. "May I ask if your client is aware of the development application that has been granted to the people who own the farmhouse next door? Do you know that if the consent is ratified by the tribunal they intend to extend the size and nature of their buildings, and open a *salle d'accueil* with parking for fifty cars?"

"Indeed we are aware of that, and I have already made myself familiar with the proposal by the LeBlanc family."

"And does that not concern your client?"

"Not at all. In fact my client may well use those facilities from time to time himself as he is frequently involved in conferences and other large gatherings. He is, one might say, a potential buyer of a kind you would not in these circumstances find it easy to come across. Many others would probably be deterred by what might be built next door."

"Well, we are certainly interested in selling," said Pru, "so let us meet with your client and discuss the matter further. Would you like to bring him here or would you prefer if we came to Toulouse? That might be better as we would want our lawyers present. But first, may we know the name of your client?"

"I fear I cannot tell you that, Madame, as the purchase would be made by a company and my client insists on total anonymity. I have his full authority to act on his behalf, including the purchase itself. But I would be happy to meet with you and your lawyers in Toulouse. Now I will thank you for your hospitality and leave you my card. Please feel free to call me at any time."

Monsieur Demey stood up, bowed to his hosts, and pulled out of the driveway as Pru was writing down the Citroen's licence plate on the back of his business card.

"Now for a bit of sleuthing," she said to Mark as they sat down for another cup of coffee. Pru looked at the card again. "A very new one I would say, just his name, a post office box and a phone number. No mention of his real estate business."

But sleuthing would have to wait. They had a concert to produce in three days' time.

12.

SUMMER MUSIC

THE idea of giving a summer concert at the château had been discussed with Dr Antoine Lefevre, who was now a close friend and frequent visitor to the château. It was decided that the ideal performance group would be a piano quartet that included Pru on piano, Antoine on cello, two of his friends on violin and viola, and possibly a vocalist, such as Adilah Ricard. The concert would be held in early July, either in a marquee on the terrace or inside in the hall, depending on the weather.

Antoine brought his cello to the château one afternoon and he and Pru delighted the family with an impromptu performance. They found that they worked well together and started to discuss a program. Pru invited Adilah to join them one afternoon and she proved to have a melodic, light soprano voice. Adilah brought along the scores for some French repertoire and they agreed on a few songs that suited her voice and would, in Pru's opinion, please their audience. But she suggested a few practice sessions as Adilah had rarely sung in public.

Three days before the concert an *Autan* – the fierce wind coming off the Mediterranean and funnelling westwards between the southern parts of the Massif Central and the

LE CHÂTEAU

Pyrenees – sprang up and was forecast to continue. Jenny, who was in charge of everything except the music, therefore decided to hold the concert in the hall. Bouquets were attached to the stone uprights on the staircase and flowers were placed in vases around the room. When the hire chairs arrived they were arranged in two quarter-circles at the bottom of the wide staircase, where four steps led up to a small landing. The piano was placed to the left and the strings were to be seated in front of the stairs. Adilah would give her performance up on the landing so she could maintain eye contact with Pru and be visible to everyone.

The stage was set, and on the day of the performance the string players arrived shortly before Adilah. Pru led them through a brief rehearsal, "more of a warm-up really", she said. They had held a complete rehearsal the night before, which was well received by those staying in the château. The performers then retired to the dining room, which doubled as a dressing room for the day.

Bernard was in charge of parking to make sure that cars could depart without delay after the concert, and François was on duty at the château gates as guests started arriving at three-thirty. The mayors of both Castres and Saint Audan had accepted, but not Christian de Montfort, who cited a previous engagement. Pru and Mark had considered inviting Yvette too but decided not to, as she was now in poor health and living some distance away.

At four o'clock Mark asked everyone to be seated, ushered in the musicians, and introduced Antoine to deliver the welcoming speech.

"Distinguished guests, *Mesdames et Messieurs,* we are honoured today by the presence of not one but two mayors," Antoine beamed. "Firstly I would like to welcome my good friend, the mayor of Castres, Pierre Combes, and his lovely wife, Angèle. We believe that this is your first visit to the Château du Moulin, and we thank you both for joining us and hope you enjoy the experience of listening to the music in such a beautiful place. We also welcome another visitor from outside this commune, Doctor Alain Frugier, who, as we know, is one of France's most respected historians and a celebrated chronicler of our times. Thank you for joining us, Doctor. And of course our second mayor needs no introduction, our own Michel Ricard, who is here with his charming wife Adilah, who will be singing for us."

Antoine extended a hand towards Adilah, who smiled and inclined her head graciously to the audience's polite greeting. She was wearing a full-length evening dress of rose-pink silk and Mark was reminded of seeing her in less formal attire of a similar colour not so long ago.

Antoine pointed to Jérome on violin and Tony on viola, saying what a pleasure it was to play with his two colleagues, and then introduced the hosts.

"We must thank the owners of this fabulous château for making our concert possible, Monsieur Mark Escott and his wife Madame Prudence, who will be joining us on piano. Also Monsieur and Madame Burlington, and the other members of their family who are present, in particular Sir Robert and Lady Ann Williams. Thank you all for being here."

Antoine led the audience in in the clapping.

"Now to our program," he said, "which we hope you will find pleasure in hearing. You will recognise most of these works which we have chosen because they celebrate the summer, or because they were written by great French composers. We shall begin with the third movement of Vivaldi's *Four Seasons*, which is, of course, *Summer*."

After a quick tuning the trio played a spirited version and bowed to the enthusiastic applause. A very good start, thought Mark. Antoine invited Pru to the piano and introduced the next piece.

"We shall now play something for you by Brahms, his Piano Quartet Number One in G minor opus 25, which was first performed in 1861 with Clara Schumann on piano. Today we entrust that task to Prudence Escott."

More applause followed a good rendition of this quite difficult piece, and Pru and Antoine were equally relieved.

"And now it is the turn of Adilah Ricard to entertain us," Antoine said with more animation in his voice. "Accompanied by Prudence, she will sing the first song in the cycle *Les nuits d'été* by Hector Berlioz. This piece is well-known in the French repertoire since it was performed and recorded by our beloved Régine de Créspin many years ago. It is entitled *Le spectre de la rose. Mesdames . . .*"

Adilah came forward and walked up the four steps on the staircase. She looked ravishing and smiled at the audience before turning to her accompanist and inclining her head. All eyes were on Adilah when she began to sing – except Toby's. He was looking at the guests to gauge their reaction. Then he watched her slowly turn her head, seeming to make eye contact with everyone in the audience until her gaze rested on Antoine as she drained the emotion from a poignant song of love lost and love refound. Antoine held her gaze, and Toby noted a bead of perspiration forming above his lip.

"By God," he hissed to Jenny, "they're in love."

The audience appreciated her singing and Adilah smiled as she announced her next song, *Après Un Reve* by Gabriel Fauré. The château itself almost seemed to sigh in harmony as music wafted out to the garden and leaves fluttered gently on the plane trees. After more applause Adilah took a bow and went back to her seat next to her husband.

Antoine introduced the final piece, the Piano Quartet in C minor opus 15, also composed by Fauré and first performed in 1877. The guests were so enchanted that they demanded an encore, and the musicians obliged with another polished excerpt from Brahms. As the applause died down Antoine thanked the audience and announced that everyone was invited to stay and enjoy the refreshments.

They filed outside to trestle tables filled with wine, beer, soft drinks and delicious *canapés* that Jenny had put together that morning. Most of the guests were happy to stay, and small groups wandered around the terrace and the garden, which was perfumed by the roses enjoying the sunlight and easing gusts of wind that signalled the end of the *Autan*.

"We are so lucky," Pru said when she emerged from the dressing room in a pretty summer dress and found her husband chatting with a group which included the two mayors.

"*Mès felicitations, Madame,*" said Pierre Combes, the mayor of Castres. "I had no idea we had so much wonderful talent in our *département*. May I offer also my most sincere thanks to you, your fellow musicians and your family for inviting us to join you on such a wonderful occasion. You have even managed to stop the *Autan!* And may I offer my congratulations to my brother mayor on having such a beautiful and gifted wife."

Adilah had joined them too after changing into a silk ensemble with pink roses, the colour that perfectly suited her complexion. She smiled and offered her cheeks to the mayor.

"Thank you, Pierre, you are most generous, and it is wonderful to see you here with Angèle," Adilah said. "For me it was a wonderful experience, and I thank you also, Michel, for supporting me in my attempts to sing."

She kissed her husband on both cheeks.

Another group chatting nearby included Sir Robert and Alain Frugier and the three string players. The OB had successfully begged a scotch from Alice while the others were drinking wine.

"Tell me," said Sir Robert, "why is it that France enjoys and displays such a wealth of musical talent while we in Great Britain seem almost shy of ours? I'm talking about what used to be called classical music. I must admit we seem to have an inexhaustible supply of pop creativity, but here in France most towns of even a modest size put on concerts. Take Castres. In the summer they give free ones in the streets as well as international dance extravaganzas, and in the winter there are Sunday evening concerts in the municipal theatre. And those performances engage the best of French talent. In England that simply does not happen."

"You make a very interesting point, Sir Robert," Frugier conceded. "And I would, with all due deference, suggest the same with regard to the visual arts. England has given birth to some wonderful composers – Tallis, Byrd, Elgar and Britten, to name but four – and visual artists too. Who could overlook Gainsborough and Turner? But where I think the English have always excelled is in the literary world. Perhaps that is a metaphor for the English character: reserved in that you do not want to put yourself on public display, but are nevertheless seeking a way to express yourselves. We French have had and still have some marvellous poets. Think only of Verlaine, Baudelaire and Victor Hugo. But we could not put up one of them to match Shakespeare, Milton and Wordsworth. I also would suggest, as an historian, that the British aristocracy have not supported classical music to the extent that it has been traditionally favoured by the elite here in Europe. In the seventeenth and eighteenth centuries, many if not most of the great European composers were supported and encouraged by kings and princes, often quite competitively, while the era of Bach produced only one exceptional English composer, Henry Purcell."

"What about Handel?" the OB suggested.

"There you go," Alain chirped, "you even have to dig up Georg Friedrich, a man born in Germany who only became English in mid-life. I will grant you that most of Handel's best known and loved works were inspired by his association with the English royal family, but do not forget the Germanic connection – they themselves were Hanoverians."

"Damn," said the OB to the musicians who were enjoying the joke. "Don't ever argue over history with this man. Or any other subject, come to that."

Meanwhile, Toby and Jenny had joined the group with the mayors and their wives, as well as others with whom they were not familiar. That didn't deter Toby.

"So, politics," he said, diving in. "How do we all feel about the result of the Brexit referendum?"

There was a pause before Pierre Combes spoke up.

"I believe that most Europeans are saddened but not surprised that a majority in the *Royaume Uni* voted to leave," he said. "You have never embraced the political reasons for the EU, being of course the elimination of yet another European war, and have only been interested in being members for access to the huge market which the twenty-eight countries in our union offer. Your governments and your media have consistently adopted a mistrustful attitude towards the EU, and increasingly towards its leadership."

"I totally agree," said Toby. "We have for centuries held onto this image of an island nation and the seductive myth of Britain standing alone: 'This royal throne of kings, this sceptred isle– '"

"'This happy breed of men, this little world, this precious stone set in a silver sea,'" Alain chimed in, completing the verse as his group merged with Toby's. "'That England that was wont to conquer others hath made a shameful conquest of itself.'"

"Well done, Alain," said the OB. "I couldn't have put it better myself."

Those who had understood laughed but some looked blank, so Toby tried to explain.

"Shakespeare wrote those lines, oh, four hundred years ago, about an England of two hundred years before that. And even then there were people looking back to a golden age which had never really happened."

"Perhaps," said Pierre, "that was because some people – maybe most people – felt dissatisfied with the world they saw about them. It is like that now. Great inequalities exist in France despite our national motto: *liberté, égalité, fraternité*. We also live with a great hypocrisy. We think of ourselves as brave revolutionaries always prepared to man the barricades to protect our hard-won rights, but at the same time there are few countries, certainly in Europe, which are as conservative as ours. We resist change."

"So, Pierre, what does the average French voter think of your president?" asked Jenny.

"This is not difficult to answer. Hollande was elected on promises to do many things and has achieved almost nothing. People have not been upset by what he has done, but by what he has not done. An almost perfect example of the French character. In 2012, Monsieur Hollande presented himself as the perfect antidote to the 'bling', I think you call it, of President Sarkozy. He was serious, cautious and very conservative in a way even French socialists can be."

"Well on a lighter note, I have a question for Madame

Combes," Jenny said. "What did you think a couple of years ago when your President was photographed on the way to his lover's apartment?"

"*Naturellement,* we expect our President to have a mistress – at least one and maybe more," Madame Combes shot back approvingly. "But what we found *déplorable* was that he was on the back of a motor scooter. That is just so undignified, and we *Françaises* lost all respect for him."

Toby started it so he had to finish it, saying, "Well thank you all very much, I think that's enough politics for one day." There were relieved smiles all round and the group broke up as they went to refresh their glasses.

"A great success I think," Mark said to Pru as they walked arm-in-arm among the trees. After playing and then trying to cope with so many conversations in French, she was feeling tired. "Is there anywhere in the world more peaceful than this?" she mused, before realising they should rejoin their guests as most people, including the mayors, were leaving.

While saying their thanks and *au revoir,* the Combes proposed inviting the Escotts and Burlingtons to their home for dinner.

"We will not suggest a date just now," Pierre said, "but let us make it during the summer holidays. We are going down to our beach house near Saint Tropez for a few days and will back by the beginning of August. I will telephone you. Until then, *merci* and *au revour.*"

They shook hands before the mayor of Castres and his wife drove away. Congratulations and thanks were also exchanged with the Ricards and Antoine, as well as his musician friends, leaving only Alain Frugier and the family out on the terrace.

"You are in danger of becoming celebrities," Frugier said. "Not only are you in the media through your dealings with

Chinese developers, you are providing culture to French people – on their own soil!"

The château, like its inhabitants, must have felt a great sense of relief that the afternoon had been so pleasant and successful, worth all the effort that had gone into it. Everyone agreed to finish off Jenny's *canapés* for dinner, so they brought chairs out to the trestle tables and sat down to enjoy the last hours before sunset. Right now, the Escotts and Burlingtons cared not what the future might hold in the fight to protect their very own slice of French paradise. For them, it was enough just being here as the day turned into a lovely evening that was cooling slightly, with only a whisper of breeze.

13.

FOLLOW THAT CAR

THE following day, however, it was time to get back to the business at hand.

The family lunched together with the staff as a way of thanking them for their assistance with the concert. Sitting in the sunshine under the trees and drinking a very palatable Gaillac *rosé* from Mas Pignou which accompanied a *filet de porc* stuffed with dates, it took some effort to confront the thought that their tranquillity was being threatened by their neighbours, perhaps also by persons unknown.

"Our one lead," said Chris, "seems to be the car. The one that man who tried to get us to sell the château to his un-named client was driving. Demey, wasn't it? Why don't you and I go into Toulouse and have a chat with your *notaire*, Dad, and see what he can turn up?"

At three p.m. the following afternoon Chris and Mark were sitting in Maitre Buffard's office, in those shiny, leather-upholstered chairs so beloved by the legal profession throughout the world.

"Whilst it is always a great pleasure to see you, and particularly to meet a young man in my own profession, I think you have come to ask me something," Maitre Buffard said. "How may I help you, gentlemen?"

Christopher responded. "And it is a pleasure and a privilege to meet you, sir. What we want to do is trace the owner of a car. We know the make and its registration – sorry, *immatriculation* – number."

"Have you been in an accident? It is usually only necessary to report the details to the police and they will carry out the search."

"No, an accident is not involved."

Mark explained the circumstances and the need to identify the owner of the Citroen discreetly.

"So is there some sort of database we can access where the details of all French vehicles are entered?" he asked Buffard.

"Aaahh, now I am following you," the notaire said. "I am not certain, but I think the database you seek is called the *Système d'Immatriculation des Véhicules*, SIV for short. I know that one can use this to make changes to one's own driving licence and other documents, but I think to check on another vehicle one must be a *professionnel*, such as an insurer or a dealer in used cars. I have friends in that milieu – *mon Dieu!* I spend much of my life keeping them out of trouble! So I will make enquiries and let you know what I find. I must warn you though that it is now very near the end of July. The schools, how do you say, break up this week and our long French summer holiday commences. I will find out what I can quickly, but maybe the full details will not be so easy. I beg you to be patient."

Patience was not a virtue, according to the Escott family, but with no option they thanked Maitre Buffard cordially, shook hands and drove back to Saint Audan.

***

It was the last Friday in July when they heard from Buffard by email: "The vehicle in which you are interested belongs to a not-for-profit association which concerns itself with the acquisition and exhibition of works of art. It is registered in the *departement* of Tarn and Garonne and is directed by a M. Philippe Suchet. I am about to go *en vacances* for two weeks, but when I get back I will make some further enquiries as to who are the principal people and organisations behind the association. Enjoy the sunshine."

"Well I wonder if Messieurs Suchet and Demey have anything in common?" Mark said to Chris. "We could do a bit of research ourselves, but I don't want to alert either of them – if indeed there are two – so perhaps we better wait a while."

"Interesting," Chris replied. "I read somewhere that the not-for-profit sector here is undergoing a bit of scrutiny. Probably long overdue, just as it should be in lots of countries that give donors tax relief. I'll have a look at the provisions relating to the governance of associations so we'll know what we're looking at when we hear from Buffard again."

Two days later Lucy arrived with Yves, bringing exciting news. Although Yves had worked at The Hotel for only five months, he was on the up and up. The Chef was so impressed by his skills and energy that she wanted him to supervise the imminent renovation of a one-star Michelin restaurant in a small town near Montauban which she had acquired a controlling interest in, and run it from the reopening in September until Christmas. She would be coming over once a fortnight to check on the progress, and Yves' job in London would be saved for him until the three of them decided whether a permanent move to France was the preferred option. The Chef had also given Yves a pay rise and a car allowance in line with the promotion, and tomorrow he and Lucy were due to meet the restaurant staff and the team doing the renovations.

"Do you think we could stay in the château for the next five months?" Lucy asked her father. "It would be lovely to spend the time here and easier for Yves to commute."

"Well for Mum and me it's not a problem," her father said, turning to Mark and Pru. "What say you?"

"It could be very useful to have a member of the family here who is French and could be in touch with our *notaire* and *avocat* if necessary. And anyway, of course you can," Mark declared on behalf of his wife.

Yves was flattered and proud to be referred to as a member of the family.

"Thank you for making me feel so much at home," he said, blushing.

On visiting La Table Aux Platanes, Yves found The Chef's new restaurant appealing and the rejuvenation work formidable. Located in a street running parallel to the main road, the restaurant was set on a sizeable block with ample parking. There were tables for sixty inside, and a sunny terrace seated another forty patrons who could dine *al fresco* in the shade of the plane trees that gave the restaurant its name.

The staff were lined up to greet Yves and Lucy, and a middle-aged man with snowy-white hair and a moustache stepped forward.

"*Bienvenu, Madame et Monsieur,*" he smiled. "Welcome. My name is Emile and I am your *maitre d'*. May I present to you firstly your kitchen staff. This is Hugo, your first *sous-chef*, and Eric, who is responsible for sauces and desserts. Then we have Dorothea who helps with the preparation – prepping, I think you call it – and is the *plongeuse*. She has been washing up for us for nearly thirty years."

Everyone shook hands and murmured a greeting.

"Next, your waitresses, Carole, Esmé and Chantal, who are with us full-time," Emile said, moving along the line. "We also have several part-timers on call. At the moment we lack one vital member of staff, a receptionist who can answer the telephone, take the bookings and maintain the computer. It is central to our system of taking the orders on a keypad, transferring them to the kitchen and producing the bills for the diners. The previous receptionist was the owner of the restaurant, so we must discuss how we should proceed in replacing her." He looked at Lucy. "I think you would be very good at greeting guests, if I may so, *Madame*."

Lucy smiled. "You are very charming, Emile, but you would have to discuss that with the boss."

"Mais certainement, Madame."

They inspected the dining room where new seating was being installed, *banquettes* along the walls and booths in the centre. The heavy tables here could be repositioned for different configurations, while out on the terrace, folding tables and chairs could accommodate bigger groups of diners. Lucy was pleased to see that the interior lighting was softly effective, enhancing the beige upholstery. In contrast, the kitchen was a shambles.

"Oh my God!" Lucy exclaimed as she walked in. The old appliances had been disconnected and the benches dismantled, leaving a huge pile of debris awaiting removal.

"This is going to be a challenge," said Yves, and he asked to see the plans for the new installation.

While Yves went over the blueprint with the kitchen staff, Lucy, Emile and the three waitresses went out to the terrace and sat down.

"I can only offer you coffee or tea and some biscuits, *Madame*," Emile said.

"Let's share some coffee, Emile. And I would like you all to call me Lucy."

Two hours later they were on their way back to the château, Lucy driving and Yves thinking. Lucy broke the silence.

"So how do you feel now about taking it on?"

Yves took his time to reply as they drove past vineyards and apple farms where the trees were tightly packed together and protected by rainproof sheeting, which also deflected the fierce August sun.

"Well, it is a big challenge," he said eventually, "but if Chef feels I can do it, bring it on, as you like to say. My first concern is whether the kitchen can be finished by the end of this month. The main contractor tells me yes, but we know French workers – they like their holidays and they like them in August. I will make my report and suggest that Chef comes over early next week and we all meet again on site."

"And what about Emile's suggestion?" she asked.

"*Pardon?* What was that?"

"That I take on the role at reception."

"Would you really want to do that? I thought you were looking forward to a long *congé* – leave."

"I would rather spend it with you," Lucy said, taking a hand off the wheel to squeeze his leg.

The Chef was delighted with the progress when she arrived for her first inspection, and everything was agreed to, including Lucy's employment at the front desk. Then Lucy returned to London with Yves to collect their possessions while he wrapped up his job at The Hotel.

***

August was fast disappearing and the family gathered at the château were finding it all too easy to just sit in the sun, swim, go for a walk as the evenings shortened, and enjoy the food and wine. They heard and saw little of their neighbours, and most of their acquaintances in the commune were either on holiday or entertaining children and grandchildren.

On the last day of the month Maitre Buffard telephoned Mark. "I have enjoyed a very pleasant holiday with my wife and our family, and since getting back I have been doing a bit more, how you say, sleuthing. I must say I did not comprehend before that the world of associations was so under-regulated. The laws go back to 1901 and it does not appear that they have been much modified since then. Any two or more people can form an association and declare it is for a non-profit objective. They may not distribute any profits, but persons or organisations making donations may receive tax deductions, and although they must publish a list of members these can be corporate bodies.

"So it is not always easy to discover exactly who is behind them, Mark. In the case of this one, it is set up to establish a regional centre for the visual arts. It is registered as *L'Association Pour Les Arts Aux Midi-Pyrenées*. I will do some more sleuthing into their list of members and perhaps you can make your own researches also."

"Thank you for your detective work, Maitre Buffard. *A bientot*," Mark said.

He looked up *L'Association Pour Les Arts Aux Midi-Pyrenées*. It appeared to have twenty-two members, some individuals, some corporate, and was run by Philippe Suchet. No annual report was available online and the next annual general meeting wasn't scheduled until February.

"If we want to beat them we better join them," Mark said, so he, Chris and Toby set up a dummy company dealing in antiques from a fictitious address in Toulouse, applied for membership of APAMP, and made a modest donation. Then they sat back and waited.

***

Everyone except Lucy and Yves had returned to London by early September. The renovations went without a hitch and the restaurant reopened for lunch on Saturday the third, fully booked due to the local press attention. Business was brisk from the outset, Yves had the kitchen humming, and Lucy was happily ensconced at the front desk.

During one busy lunchtime she phoned him to come to reception urgently.

"The two men on table five called for the bill and one paid with a credit card in the name of Philippe Suchet," Lucy said as she was looking in their direction. "Am I right in thinking that rings a bell? Emile says they're regulars."

Yves left the kitchen, gave Lucy a peck on the cheek, and went out to the terrace, where the lunch crowd were finishing their dessert and coffee. He walked around as chefs do, asking the diners if everyone was satisfied with their *repas*. The two men on table five, both middle-aged and wearing expensive suits, said "*Oui*," and the shorter one tapped his belly as they got up to leave.

Three minutes later Yves was back in the kitchen and on the phone to Mark.

"I have a surprise for you," he said. "We have just had two guests who are regulars. One was Philippe Suchet. Lucy identified him from his credit card. I am sure I recognised the other one, a taller man, although I have only seen him once before, at the lunch at the fete last year when I met you all. It was Christian de Montfort."

There were a few seconds of silence.

"This is all beginning to make sense, Yves," Mark said. "Well done. I will call you back at the château when I've talked to Toby and Chris. And thank you. Thank you very much. You and Lucy are definitely the right people in the right place. I shall see you soon."

***

On his next Monday off Yves sought out his distant and much older cousin-in-law, François Bardou, a farmer who lived with his son, Jean-Claude, the one who had first alerted Mark Escott to the planning application by the LeBlancs after meeting him at one of the other summer fetes. It was a glorious day, the sunflowers had just been harvested, and Jean-Claude was preparing to bring in the last of their summer crops, the corn. Yves sat on the grass near the farmhouse with François while drinks were fetched by Angelique, his daughter-in-law.

Yves told Francois about the shenanigans with the LeBlancs and Christian de Montfort's appearance at the restaurant with Philippe Suchet, and asked him if de Montfort could be the one scheming to acquire the Château du Moulin.

"And why would the mayor help him, Francois? Is it for money? Michel Ricard does not seem to be short of it."

The old man stroked his chin, deep in thought, before replying.

"I see that I must tell you something that has only been known to a few families for a very long time, more than seventy years in fact. I have to take you back to 1943 when the German invaders began to see they were not winning the war. They were suffering terrible losses in Russia and their workforce was being depleted daily as more and more men were sent to the front line. Hitler's industrialists under Albert Speer demanded that more of our young men be conscripted to work in their labour camps, and each city, town and village in France was given a quota. This is when collaboration really started."

"Yes, I remember that from the school lessons about the war."

"Pétain was being totally ignored by the senior Germans. They only dealt with Laval, who was by then head of the government, and he used the French authorities to implement the quotas. Vichy France was under direct German control, so the quotas became the job of officials in the *Mairies* – not an enviable job, but one they could not avoid if they themselves were not to be deported. So they made choices about who to send away, and in this commune one of those chosen was Jean-Michel Ricard, who was eventually to be the father of our mayor. Jean-Michel was eighteen, and his father fought his deportation. He got in touch with his friend in Paris, Xavier de Montfort, and they did a terrible deal which involved my family. Xavier took Jean-Michel's name off the list and substituted the name of Eric Bardou . . . my older brother. Eric was soon on his way to a labour camp. He did not survive there long. He was chronically sick with tuberculosis, which was probably why his name was not on the original list, and he died early in 1944."

"*Mon Dieu!*" exclaimed Yves, who had turned pale. "So your family has lived in silence with this for all this time. But how does it explain—"

"It explains much," François said. "In return, the family Ricard promised to do anything, everything ever demanded of it by the de Montforts. It explains why Michel Ricard gave his new wife to Christian to be his mistress, which was widely known but not understood by our commune. And it may explain why he has signed the development consent for your family's neighbours. Had it not been for Jean-Claude's intervention, the time for an objection by Monsieur Escott might have lapsed and the family – your family – would be facing a huge loss in the value of the property. I am telling you this now because I am an old man and I have waited more than seventy years to have some sort of revenge on de Montfort because his father conspired to kill my brother. Now is the time for you to do what you think is right, Yves. I am sorry, but I am tired and I have to rest. I can say no more."

Yves kissed the old man, thanked him and left. Mark was arriving from London later that afternoon and he would hear the whole disgraceful story.

14.

CHRISTMAS IN FRANCE

JENNY, Toby, Sarah and Tom, with their sixteen-month old baby, joined Lucy and Yves in France for Christmas while the Escotts stayed in London to entertain Robert and Ann, who were finding travelling quite difficult, especially the OB, who was turning eighty-four in March.

The Burlingtons arrived three days before Christmas Day and were delighted to find two trees in the hall and the sitting room, beautifully decorated by Alice, Bernard and François, who had also surpassed themselves with the external lighting which was sparkling all over the front of the château.

On Christmas Eve, Yves and Lucy returned from an exhausting day at work just in time for a glass of midnight champagne before going to bed. After working non-stop for four months since the reopening they had earned a few days off. La Table Aux Platanes was pleasing everyone, especially the new owner in London. With good reviews in the press and social media, they were confident of retaining its one-star Michelin rating.

In line with the family tradition, the presents were opened while sitting around the tree after breakfast on Christmas Day.

Lunch was scheduled for one o'clock, a free-range turkey that Jenny and Sarah bought from a neighbouring farmer and stuffed with sage and onion, combined with a hock of ham. The only guest at lunch was Antoine, who arrived on his own.

"I have some news," Lucy said as they were sitting by the fire after lunch. "Yves has asked me to marry him."

Her father smiled. "Lucy, that is wonderful news and a fantastic Christmas present for us all to share." He got up to embrace his daughter and Yves, who was blushing in happiness. "And I suppose you said yes?"

"Very quickly," Lucy laughed. "Didn't give him time to change his mind."

"Well done! We are *so* happy," said Jenny, and everyone got up to hug the loving couple. "Have you got a date in mind?"

"We're thinking of Easter and getting married here in Saint Audan, just a civil ceremony and lunch, and having the reception at the restaurant. We haven't asked the staff or the owner yet, but we think they might agree."

After more talk about wedding plans the conversation petered out and they sat there watching the flames in the huge stone fireplace. Eventually Antoine took a deep breath and spoke up.

"I would like to share some news with you too. It is not so exciting and lovely as Lucy's, but for me it will be life-changing. Early in the new year I am giving up my doctor's practice."

They looked at him, perplexed.

"This certainly is a surprise, Antoine," Jenny said. "And I'm not sure whether it is good news or bad news . . . for you, I mean."

"Well, I will give you the reasons and then perhaps you can judge, but for me I think it is a necessary step forward, although not everything will be easy. May I say you will be the only people to whom I have talked until things are settled. There are several reasons for giving up the practice. I have been a general practitioner for more than twenty years and I need to change. But more importantly, the other reason which I will come to may cause me to face a charge of unprofessional conduct."

They all looked aghast.

"For many years I have been having an affair with a married woman who came to me for medical treatment. She has now agreed to leave her husband, which is what I most dearly wish, but she agrees with me that we could not continue with our lives in Castres, where my home is. And so I have been offered and will accept a position in the headquarters of Pierre Fabre near Lavaur, where I can continue to use my medical skills but avoid *la scandale.*"

"And I think this will cause quite a stir in Saint Audan too, if I'm not mistaken," Toby said.

Antoine's shoulders went back as if he had received a blow.

"What do you mean?" he asked, his voice shaking.

"I mean that the lady in question lives in Saint Audan," Mark said.

Antoine looked confused. "How do you know that? Has she talked to you?"

"She didn't need to, Antoine. We saw how you looked at each other at the concert here in July."

"*Mon Dieu!* If you have guessed, how many others too?"

"Perhaps not many," said Mark, "but in a small *commune* like this it seems that everyone knows everyone else's business."

Antoine averted his eyes in embarrassment before speaking again.

"I am so glad I have shared this with you, my friends, and I hope that we shall continue to be friends when Adilah and I are finally together. These last few years have been hell for both of us, but particularly for her. Sadly there is little love, not even respect, between Adilah and Michel. In fact she is frightened of him and what he might do to her and to the children, although Louisa is now living away from home and has a good job. But we are worried about Laurent, who is at a critical age with many decisions ahead of him. We know he is interested in the development of the medical sciences and I shall certainly be available to help him if he wants it. *On verra*. We shall see."

Jenny broke the silence that followed.

"I have one question," she said. "Who the hell is going to replace you as our GP?"

It was a good question at the right moment and Antoine laughed.

"Don't worry," he said. "I will find someone really good for you. Someone who doesn't come to your Christmas parties to embarrass himself."

Toby refilled their glasses and they drank to happy days in the year ahead.

15.

CHRISTMAS IN ENGLAND

MARK, Pru, Christopher, Diane, Chloe and Joey joined Ann and the OB for Christmas at their spacious late-Victorian house just off the upper Richmond Road in Putney. They brought along provisions for a two-day stay, leaving the cooking to the girls while the OB looked after the liquid intake, putting a lifetime of practice to excellent use for the festive season.

The presents were displayed around the big tree that Ann had decorated, and the grandchildren were entranced as they counted down the hours to Christmas Day.

The weather in London was as bad as Saint Audan, but because of the city's prohibition on open indoor fires dating back to the nineteen sixties it had to be central heating keeping everyone warm at the OB's place, unlike the château where the hearth was ablaze.

Following a late supper on Christmas Eve they planned to walk to the midnight carol service at St Mary's at the foot of Putney Bridge, which dated back to medieval times. After being torched by an arsonist in the nineteen seventies it reopened in 1982, and was now a beautiful mixture of modern materials used to recreate a comfortable but ancient environment.

The church visit was a first for the children, as Pru noted when they set off. "I haven't been in a church since Joey was christened, and I'm still not quite sure why we even did that. I'm afraid my belief in all this stuff has been pretty much knocked out of me. Mark and I never go to church these days."

"I still do pretty often, but these days it's usually for a funeral," Robert said. "My old mates are dropping off the perch. It will be nice to be there for something a bit more bloody cheerful."

The service was much more than cheerful. Eight carols were sung by choir and congregation, interspersed with readings from the four Books of the Apostles. Believers and unbelievers alike were buoyed by the words and the music, and the children were spellbound.

On Christmas morning Chloe and Joey woke late to stockings filled with goodies and a couple of presents each from Ann and the OB: two changes of clothes for Chloe's favourite doll and two remote-control toy cars for Joey. Chloe joined grandma in bed while Joey sat on the bedroom floor, getting grandpa to fetch his cars and having a great time.

It was nearly ten when everyone assembled for a light breakfast. At noon Alain Frugier arrived to join them in the family tradition of Christmas lunch, and after the exchange of gifts Robert opened an extremely expensive champagne for a toast.

"So what have you been up to?" Robert asked Alain.

"I am working on a new book, *mon ami*, a history of anti-semitism over two thousand years. I am attempting to link this with the rise of nationalism which appears to be coinciding with its resurgence in many countries."

"Sounds interesting. Will you be exclusively dealing with anti-semitism in the West or will you be looking at anti-semitism in

Muslim countries too?"

"I will try to show that the two are different. In the Middle East I think I can demonstrate that the prejudice is racial, whereas in the West it has usually been an outlet for expressing a reaction to other fears, such as it was in France about a communist takeover in the mid-nineteen thirties."

"Interesting," Robert repeated. "And it seems to be a particularly Christian reaction. Do you think those passages in the gospels telling of Jesus overturning the tables and throwing out the moneylenders from the temple have anything to do with it? I mean when I was at school those passages, particularly the ones in Saint Matthew, were used time and time again in sermons, often in conjunction with the idea that it was more blessed to give than to receive. We used to come out of chapel and give the few Jews in our school a hard time, I can tell you."

"You have my point exactly, Sir Robert," said Alain. "It is always comforting to find someone inferior to oneself. That piece of history – or certainly folklore – has become so embedded in Christian tradition that it is regarded as a justified act, whereas some of us might now think it was an act of unprovoked aggression."

"You're too damned right, Alain. When I got out of school, started thinking for myself and got on the bench, I asked what I would have done if a young man had done that and come up before me on charges of assault and causing an affray. He would have got thirty days for a first offence and been bound over from entering temples. Can't let people get away with that sort of behaviour."

"So much for the peaceful Christmas message," said Pru, rolling her eyes. "Let's eat."

16.

THE ASSOCIATION FOR THE ARTS IN THE MIDI-PYRENEES

FEBRUARY arrived and the day for the annual general meeting of the Association for the Arts in the Midi-Pyrenees was drawing close.

Mark, Chris and Toby had elected to attend and ask some questions, but they had no way of knowing what to expect. They were only advised by email that the meeting would be held in a hotel near Toulouse airport, starting at eleven-thirty a.m. After parking their car they split up and went inside separately at one-minute intervals to avoid drawing attention.

Mark walked into the meeting room last, wearing tinted glasses and leaving his soft hat on until he took a seat at the back, well away from Chris and Toby. The two men on the head table were deep in conversation, paying no attention to the twenty-odd people in attendance. Two paintings were positioned on easels beside them. Toby was sitting two rows up from Mark, and Chris, as planned, was in the front row. If questions were taken, he was their man. On the other side of the room Mark spotted their adviser, Maitre Buffard.

Even for the AGM of a not-for-profit association the process seemed remarkably informal. Nobody had asked Mark or the others for their name or their interest in being there and no agenda papers had been handed out. To Mark it all seemed a bit un-French.

Finally, the two men on the top table looked up and the meeting got underway.

"Mesdames et Messieurs, je m'appele Philippe Suchet and I am the chairman of your association. On my right is Monsieur Christian de Montfort, who will be well known to you both as the *Deputé* for the Tarn and as one of our region's most generous philanthropists. I will now pass you over to him."

"Thank you, Philippe," Christian de Montfort said, remaining seated. *"Mes amis,* we are happy to welcome you here today, and thank you for giving me the opportunity to report to you on the activities of the association over the past year. I have good news and some news which is not so good. On the positive side, your association has acquired several new artworks, of which these two" – he gestured to the canvasses – "we feel are very worthy examples of recent works in our region by relatively young artists. On my left is *Le Soleil sur les Tournesols* by Vincent Delprade and on my right is *Le Pic du Midi au Lever du Jour* by Pascal Pezet. Our continuing aim is to recognise the talents of former and older artists from this region, as well as to support and encourage younger members of the artistic community.

"During this last year we held a very successful competition for new works in the Grand Hotel in Toulouse and it was visited by over one thousand people. Our judging panel was comprised of two professors of art from Paris and Toulouse, as well our dear friend from the Tate Modern in London, Doctor Frank Knight. They were unanimous in awarding the first prize equally to these two paintings, which we were very happy to acquire."

A murmur of appreciation rippled through the room.

"I must thank you and many others for your generous donations and support," de Montfort continued. "Sadly, though, we have not been successful yet in finding a permanent home for our growing collection. During the year we found a house which could be perfect for a permanent exhibition but negotiations, while still continuing, have not yet come to a positive conclusion. Philippe and I hope to be able to report positively on this by the time of our next meeting. So, I thank you again for your attendance today, and we should be happy to take any questions you may have."

A young man got to his feet and read a rambling speech of congratulations. Christian de Montfort thanked him and looked at the attendees with eyebrows raised, thinking perhaps that he could close the meeting. Christopher was too quick for him.

"I represent one of your donors and I would like to ask a question," he said. "Could you tell us, *s'il vous plait,* where all the paintings are now being stored and whether you could make it possible for us to view them, as we are art lovers?"

De Montfort was taken aback by the question, but being a politician, he didn't miss a beat.

"As I have intimated, the works are not all held in one place at this time, partly for reasons of insurance and partly because it is not possible to make them available to the public. That is one of our major objectives for the next year."

"I appreciate that it is not possible to make the collection available to the public, but would it not be possible to make it accessible to members of the association from time to time by appointment?" Chris urged. "And I have another question. Would it be possible to circulate to the members a list of the artworks in the collection with the dates of purchase and the prices paid?"

The politician was right back on form.

"*Mon cher Monsieur,* these are indeed excellent suggestions, and Philippe and I will discuss urgently what we might do to satisfy your very reasonable requests. It is encouraging for us to receive such intelligent and positive ideas, especially from our new members, for which we both thank you. We should be most grateful if you would leave your name and contact details with us." De Montfort looked around the room. "I thank you all once again for coming together with us today and I will now close the meeting. Philippe and I wish you all *bon appetit et bon après-midi.*"

Mark waited for a few well-wishers to shake hands with Suchet and de Montfort on the way out before approaching them hatless and removing his tinted glasses. Suchet looked at him, trying to remember where he had seen Mark before, and de Montfort stared. His eyes glittered, just as they had when they first met nearly two years ago.

Mark smiled and extended his hand towards Suchet.

"*Bonjour*, Monsieur Suchet. Or is it Monsieur Demey today? And Monsieur de Montfort. *Bonjour aussi.* I would like to say it is a pleasure."

Mark's use of French was very good and the irony was not lost on de Montfort.

"Why are you here?" de Montfort asked.

"Well, to start with, we are members of your association," Mark replied. "But more importantly, we wanted to be sure that it is you who is attempting to get ownership of Le Château du Moulin. Now we have our proof."

By this time Toby and Chris had joined Mark and the three of them stood looking down at the two Frenchmen. Suchet was nervous, but de Montfort got up and looked Mark in the eye.

"And what will you do with your so-called proof?" he

sneered. "One day you will be begging me to buy the château at any price I choose."

"Oh, I don't think so," Mark said with a knowing smile. "If you were the last person alive with a fifty euro note I would never sell to you. You are a conniving and deceitful man. Our whole family love France and most Frenchmen and women, but you are an exception. We shall do our utmost to discredit you and undo your outrageous plans for stealing our home. And I say our home because it is now, and it has never been yours since your father died."

De Montfort's eyes glittered again like a brown snake's in the Australian bush and he looked ready to strike.

"You cannot touch me," he proclaimed. "I am a member of the French parliament and I have powerful friends in high places."

"Thinking like that is what makes you vulnerable, and being vulnerable makes you weak," Mark shot back. "Over quite a long life I have found that men in positions of authority take advantage of their apparent power to commit acts that cannot be justified." Mark was on a roll. "A close examination of your life and your actions will bring forth many things you would like to think are closely guarded secrets. *On verra, Monsieur*. As for you, Monsieur Suchet, you do not make a reliable *adjoint*. I would recommend that you reconsider your relationship with this man. *Et maintenant, messieurs, nous vous souhaitons un bon après-midi. Au revoir.*"

Mark, Chris and Toby walked out and drove off to meet Maitre Buffard at their favourite restaurant in Toulouse, Le Bibent on Place Capitole. The Maitre was there when they arrived, waiting at a secluded table.

"I spoiled myself. I hired a taxi to take me to the meeting and to wait and bring me back here. Don't worry," he said, fluffing out his hands in a deprecatory manner when Toby tried to speak, "you will find it on your next bill."

Everyone laughed.

"A lawyer after my own heart," Chris quipped.

"That was the shortest and least informative AGM I've ever been to," Mark said. "What did you make of it, *Maitre*?"

"It was interesting for those very reasons," he noted. "And the fact that Christopher was the only person who asked a question leads me to think that we were the only real members to attend. The others looked like—"

"A rent-a-crowd?" Toby interjected.

"*Exactement, mon vieux!* We have no expression in French which is so good. Rent-a-crowd is perfect. They did not look like lovers of art. As for the conduct of the meeting, well what can I say? No agenda, no financial reports, nothing."

"I've done a bit of research into not-for-profit organisations in France and they seem to fall into two main categories," Chris said. "Associations and foundations, with most by far being associations because the regulations don't seem to be all that strict. Am I right, *Maitre*?"

"You are indeed," replied Buffard. "Amazingly, it may seem to you, the law governing associations dates back to 1901 and has not been significantly changed since then. Any two or more people can form an association, and the first and most important point is that they may not benefit by way of salaries or shares of profit from its activities. Secondly, if a bank account is opened the association must be *declaré* at its local *préfecture*, but after that there are not too many demands. The benefits of an association are several. Its income is normally free from tax and people making donations to it will receive reductions in their personal tax up to a certain amount. Unsurprisingly there are hundreds of thousands of associations in France and most receive little oversight. It is probably a rock which no government will want to overturn for fear of what and who may be found under it."

"So what do you recommend, *Maitre*?" Toby asked.

"I think we should get in touch with our mutual friend and your *avocat*, Maitre Tournier. He has much more experience than me in such matters and is, if you will forgive me, more in touch with the low-life of this world. With your permission I will call him."

They nodded and Buffard hit a contact on his iPhone.

"Tournier *içi.*"

"*Bonjour*, Maitre Tournier. It is Buffard calling you and I have with me *les deux* Messieurs Escott, Mark and Christopher, and Monsieur Toby Burlinson. With your permission I would like to put you on my loudspeaker."

"A pleasure, and *bonjour à tout le monde.*"

Maitre Buffard gave his colleague a synopsis of the AGM and their wish to look more closely into the affairs of the association, in particular the role of Christian de Montfort.

"For me it is difficult to make more enquiries without giving away the identity of those I am working for, Louis. But I thought that perhaps you might have some means of looking into the affairs of de Montfort and his association, especially whether they have been following their obligations with respect to taxation. May I ask your views?"

"You have every right to hold suspicions, *mes amis*," Tournier agreed. "This whole area of French business – and I call it a business because that is what it has become – is full of tax avoidance and corruption. I have not become overly involved because it is a very specialised area, but I do have some friends, and I think now of one in particular who might help you. He is a senior member of the tax department in Toulouse and he owes me a favour. Several in fact, because I got him off a charge of attempted rape a few years ago. He was, I have to say, not guilty, but it was not easy. The young woman involved had been investigated for tax fraud and alleged that my client had proposed a deal and, when she refused, he tried to have sex with her anyway. It was one person's word against another's, but fortunately for my client there was a leak to the media about some earlier misdoings of this young woman and the jury acquitted him. Ah, these leaks! Who knows from where they come?"

Everyone was smiling as Tournier pressed on.

"Therefore, if I may presume that you agree, I would propose that I contact this person in the tax office and see what he might be able to unearth for us. He will report off the record only to me, but I will keep you fully informed."

"Louis, we are already indebted to you. It's Mark speaking. We shall be very happy to put this matter in your capable hands. Thank you, sir."

The conversation ended, they enjoyed their meal, and after leaving the restaurant Mark and Chris flew back to London while Toby drove to the château to see his daughter.

Lucy came home early from work, leaving one of the young waitresses to operate the computer system and Emile, the *maitre d'*, with the greeting duties, for which he was perfect.

"How are the wedding plans coming along?" Toby asked as he gave her a hug.

"We're pretty much set," Lucy smiled. "The wedding will be at noon in the *Mairie*, and I have to say that our mayor has become so much more friendly and helpful again."

"Really? Why is that?"

"Well, I have a theory but I'll come back to that. The reception will be in the restaurant and the staff will join us when the food is served. And Madame, the proprietor, says she wants to fly over to join us on the day. Isn't that wonderful?"

"I am just so happy for you, darling. You and Yves deserve every good thing that comes your way. Mum and I are so proud of you. Is there anything we can do?"

"Just be there, Dad. And say some nice things about me in your speech."

"I'll try. Now what's this about Michel Ricard?"

"Well, ever since Adilah left him to live with Antoine, Michel seems – how can I put it – more relaxed whenever I see him. Sometimes he comes to the restaurant for a meal. You know that Laurent has now left him as well, and he's living with his mother and Antoine? It's as if a weight has been taken off Michel's shoulders. Lots of people have remarked on it. Anyway, we invited him to do the honours and he accepted."

They continued to talk about the wedding as Lucy went through the guest list, and after dinner and a nightcap with Yves when he came home they went to bed.

17.

EASTER BRIDE

AS IN the best tales about Easter brides, the sun came out for Lucy on her wedding day. In fact the weather on Saturday the fifteenth of April was perfect: warm but not too hot, with a fluky breeze to rustle the new leaves in the oaks and plane trees. The château looked on approvingly as the noon nuptials approached.

Lucy was wearing a full-length dress in white silk and a cape to cover her bare shoulders. Yves complemented her in a light-grey, three-piece suit, white shirt and grey tie. They drew admiring looks when they entered the *Mairie* arm-in-arm one minute before noon.

The room where the mayor would officiate was blooming with spring tulips, daffodils, jonquils and mimosa placed in each corner, and around the small platform installed for the ceremony. The sixty guests were seated on either side of the centre isle covered by a red carpet, and the official party occupied the front row: Lucy's sister Sarah and their grandfather, her two witnesses, Chloe the flower girl, Yves' mother, and one of his best friends from school days.

Everybody stood as Lucy and Yves entered, and Michel Ricard smiled when they stepped up to the platform in front of him. He asked the guests to be seated and delivered his welcome, direct and personal. He noted that he had known Yves since he was a baby and had the pleasure of seeing him grow into an industrious and sensitive young boy. The mayor paid great respect to Yves' mother, Anne-Marie, for raising her son on her own after the premature death of his father, who would have been so proud of him today.

Of Lucy, the mayor said it was a pleasure for him and the whole *commune* of Saint Audan to welcome her into their midst. They had only known her for two years, but she and her family had brought new life into the village, and he and his fellow councillors and friends were delighted that she had chosen a local boy as her husband, particularly as they were living in the château and working not far away. He hoped that their children would grow up happy and healthy in the community, wished them success in their careers, and called the four witnesses to step forward.

Each witness solemnly swore that the bride or groom was the person described, that to the best of their knowledge they were not already married, and that they had known them for many years. For three of the four it was since birth. The mayor pronounced them legally married and they exchanged rings and a kiss. Yves thanked him and they turned around to a wave of applause. Chloe gave Lucy the bouquet of roses she had been guarding, and the bride and groom walked back down the red carpet ahead of the witnesses, the other family members and the assembled guests.

Instead of confetti, Jenny and Pru handed out packets of dried rose petals, and after being showered by everybody the wedding party posed for photographs. Then it was off to the reception. Following the French tradition, two cars carrying friends of Yves led the cavalcade. They tooted their horns and waved out of the windows until they reached the main road for the forty-minute drive to the restaurant.

The staff were waiting on the terrace to greet and seat the wedding guests under parasols at tables of eight, except the bridal couple who had a table for sixteen. As the terrace filled to capacity, about twenty guests were accommodated inside the restaurant. Champagne corks popped and Lucy and Yves began to mingle, greeting the well-wishers they had not spoken to at the *Mairie*, including a few of Yves' friends who Lucy didn't know. Then Emile advised Toby that lunch was ready, and Toby slipped into his master of ceremony guise, asking everyone to be seated.

What a feast! The first course was *vichyssoise*, a cold cream of potato soup, and the second course was thin slices of smoked trout served with guacamole and coleslaw. For the main course Yves had chosen *filet mignon*, offering platters of rare, medium and well done. This was accompanied by a top-shelf pinot noir from Burgundy, specially chosen and paid for by Sir Robert as his contribution to the festivities. The aroma of the beef and the delicate perfume of the wine mixed perfectly with the scent of the flowers in the garden.

"Heaven can't be better than this," said Lucy, kissing her new husband.

A cheeseboard followed, consisting of *Tomme de Brebis*, a firm sheep cheese from the Savoie region, *camembert* and *roquefort* from the Auvergne, and a delightfully soft *chevre*, goat's cheese from a nearby village in the hills of the Sidobre. Every taste was catered for. After a dessert of mixed berries and cream, coffee was served with the speeches.

Following the English custom, Toby, as the bride's father, spoke first, welcoming everyone in French and recalling some of Lucy's forays into boyfriends as a teenager, making her blush.

"But it has all turned out very well indeed, and this is one of the happiest days of our lives, isn't it, my darling?" he said, turning to Jenny and kissing her hand.

Speeches by the groom and best man followed, and then Sir Robert asked if he might say a few words.

"We have never in our lives heard you say only a few words," Toby joked, "so just remember we have to be out of here before nightfall."

Sir Robert rose to his feet, smiling. "I will have to address you in English and hope that your neighbour can translate some of this if needs be. In England, I am known as the Old Bastard – *batard*, I think, in French. This is probably for several reasons, but mostly because I say what I think and don't mind to whom I'm saying it. Today we celebrate something – and two people – very close to my heart. The joining together of our beloved Lucy and Yves, whom we have come to know and respect, is wonderful. But it is also the coming together of two countries, France and England, this time in peace and love rather than in times of conflict as we have known before.

"I have had my own love affair with your country since I was a child. My father fought for us all during the Second World War and brought me and my mother to see it when I was still in my teens. I think I have passed on much of this love to my two daughters, and now to my beautiful grand-daughter, Lucy."

Lucy looked up at the Old Bastard and smiled the words "Yes, you have."

"Now before I propose a toast to the lovely couple, may I make a brief diversion. My family know that I voted for Brexit. I have always questioned the ways the European Union has been structured and the unelected autocrats who run it, but I've always supported its creation. In many respects I am deeply saddened that Great Britain is leaving, but perhaps it might make the leaders of Europe give some serious thought to the major changes the EU needs, and this thinking must start right here in France as well as in Germany.

"My dear friends – *mes amis* – you will be electing a new president over the next few weeks. For your future and your children's, I hope and pray that you will elect a person who is pro-Europe but who has the balls – *en Français courage, peut-etre* – to make those changes, and perhaps we shall find ways in Great Britain to support a new union of Europeans. Thank you for putting up with a bit of politics from me on such a happy occasion. And now I raise my glass to Lucy and Yves, and to all of you."

Toby stood up. "Well thank you, father-in-law. That must be the shortest speech you've ever made, and I'm sure that most of us here today support your feelings. One other person has asked if she may speak, and it is my great pleasure to introduce you to Eloise, who is the owner of this splendid restaurant and the employer of both Yves and Lucy, as well as a longstanding friend of Sir Robert."

"Thank you, Toby," said Eloise, The Chef. "I am so happy to be here. I have attended many weddings, frequently in a professional capacity, but rarely has one been as well organised and beautifully prepared. If I may say so, this is a beautiful venue, and on a day like this . . . well, just perfect. I particularly want to thank and congratulate Yves and his team for their success in not just maintaining but improving the high standards our restaurant is known for, and improving the bottom line financially as well." The guests applauded. "And now I would like to offer our newlyweds a gift. Not in gold or silver but in paper. In fact a certificate for ten per cent of the shares in the company which owns this restaurant. Also included is a letter setting out some suggestions as to how you might, if you wish, increase this shareholding until we become equal partners. But we shall discuss that at another time."

Eloise took the share certificate from her handbag and proudly displayed it. Yves and Lucy were speechless, but the groom rose to the occasion.

"Eloise . . . Madame Chef . . . I am almost lost for words. But, well, thank you. This is such an unexpected, indeed undreamed of moment. Firstly I am married, and then we are shareholders in this wonderful restaurant. I have always enjoyed working with you and for you, and Lucy and I and our great staff will continue to do our utmost to retain your respect. Thank you, Eloise," he said, kissing her cheek.

The staff were on their feet clapping and everyone else joined in. Emile led his team to the bridal table and they embraced Yves and Lucy before going over to Eloise and hugging her too. Eloise was radiant.

Toby wrapped up proceedings as the sun dipped behind the distant mountains, and the wedding party raised a final toast to a perfect ending on a perfect day.

The next morning, Easter Sunday, Lucy, Yves and the family, plus Alain Frugier, were assembled in the kitchen at nine o'clock when the sisters began cooking their signature breakfast dish of scrambled eggs and bacon with buttered toast and coffee.

"Help yourselves to cutlery and mugs and go into the dining room, we need some space in here," Jenny ordered, and the adults and children all obeyed.

After eating, the plates were cleared away, the coffee mugs were replenished, and Yves opened the envelope with Eloise's letter. It ran to several pages and there was a covering note from a *notaire* summarising the share proposal. Yves scanned it and passed it to his new uncle-in-law, Mark.

"You are the accountant and most likely to understand this," he said. "Could you translate it and give us your first impressions?"

Mark read through the proposal slowly and resummarised the *notaire's* comments in English.

"Essentially it is as Eloise said. The agreement is between Yves and Lucy as the first party, the company owning the property and the business as the second, and Eloise as the third. The proposal is for an agreed format depending on future retained profits. It means the company would buy back up to fifty per cent of the share capital from Eloise, so she recovers her half of the original investment. Those shares bought back would be offered to Yves and Lucy for a nominal sum while recognising their contribution to the company's earnings. It's really a bonus scheme which is not designated as such. It will take me, and I would suggest an *expert comptable,* some time to go right through the details, and I need to check that there are no hidden tax implications. But it all seems kosher and it's a very generous offer. On current levels of profitability it might take five years for you to get the other forty per cent of the shares, maybe longer, but it's a wonderful way to get started in your own business. And by the way, if you accept, Eloise would like to offer Yves a place on the board immediately."

"So, not only have I married a great chef," said Lucy, putting her arms round Yves' neck and kissing him. "I've married a great businessman. Always knew there was something about him."

18.

A NEW PRESIDENT

MOST of the family returned to London after the Easter weekend. For Chloe and Joey it was back to school, for others a return to work. Mark and Pru stayed on at the château as they were interested in observing the process of voting for a new president, and the first round was scheduled for the following Sunday.

François Hollande had declined to run again, becoming the first president of the Fifth Republic not to stand for a second term. The candidate for the traditional right-of-centre Republican Party, François Fillon, had been ahead in the opinion polls until it was revealed that he had been paying members of his family for non-existent jobs out of government funds and his ratings nosedived. At the same time, a young and little-known politician, Emmanuel Macron, had formed a new centre-right party called *En Marche!* (Let's Go!) which was doing well. As in many countries, there was a groundswell for change in France, even if few people could actually describe what that should entail.

Alain Frugier was getting animated as he and Mark shared a bottle of *rosé* from the château's climate-controlled wine cabinet while sitting under the trees at sunset.

"Look, my friend, last year in Great Britain you had the Brexit referendum, and in the United States they elected Donald Trump. There were no compelling reasons put forward to vote for Brexit or Trump, just a wave of support for the feeling that 'we want a change'. Here it is the same. After four years of Hollande, a socialist president who did nothing, a left which cannot make up its mind on what it wants, and a centre-right bloc which is seen as corrupt, it is not surprising that the frontrunners in this election are Marine Le Pen and Macron."

"But Le Pen is practically fascist, isn't she?" asked Mark.

"Well her father certainly was, but she has tried, and for some people succeeded, to distance herself from his more extreme beliefs and policies. But she is still anti-EU, anti-immigration, and considered to be anti-semitic. So are a lot of French men and women these days. We shall see on Sunday."

Mark and Alain had been invited by Michel Ricard to attend the counting of votes cast in Saint Audan, so at five forty-five p.m. on Sunday, the twenty-third of April, 2017, they drove over to the *Mairie*, which looked very different from the wedding ceremony it hosted a week ago. Today it was filled with bare tables and chairs.

Sitting behind the tables, facing the door, were several faces they recognised, mostly members of the *conseil municipal*, discussing paperwork. A late voter hurried in, showed his registration card, signed the electoral roll, and was given a handful of papers, each with the name of a candidate, plus an envelope. After coming out of the voting booth he placed the envelope in the box in front of the mayor, who depressed a lever to register that another vote had been cast.

On the dot of six o'clock the mayor declared the polling closed. Two of his assistants opened the box containing the votes, tipped the envelopes onto a table, and stacked them in piles of twenty before doing a recount.

"The totals have to equal the number of people on the roll who voted and what the counter records on the ballot box," Alain whispered.

"What happens if they don't?" Mark wondered.

"It takes a lot longer."

When the tally was complete and signed off, the ballots were transferred to another table where two other pairs of officials sat facing each other. One pair opened the envelopes and called out the names of the candidates enclosed. The other pair marked a box beside each candidate's name on large, ledger-like sheets of paper. Whenever a candidate reached a multiple of ten votes one of these scrutineers called out the figure, which his partner had to agree with. Each time twenty votes were recorded the total was compared with the tally sheets. Empty envelopes or those containing more than one vote were recorded as invalid.

It soon became evident who was winning.

"Am I hearing this right?" Mark said. "It's Le Pen well out in front, with Fillon second and Macron just holding onto third place?"

"Correct, Mark. When it is finished I will get a copy of the final scores and we can compare it tomorrow with the final count nationally. But if you didn't know it already, you're in right-wing territory here, *mon ami*."

The counting came to an end, the mayor announced the result, and invited everyone to an *apero*. Michel and his two deputies disappeared momentarily and reappeared carrying trays of glasses and bottles of *pastis* and whisky.

"Do you find democracy and our voting process so much different to what you have in England?" Michel asked Mark.

"Not so different from us, but a lot different from Australia where I spent quite a few years. Down there voting is compulsory – if you don't vote you get fined. But – and it's a big BUT – there is relatively little control of the actual process. For instance, you usually have multiple choices for polling stations where you can cast your vote, and there used to be a saying, 'vote early and vote often'." This was quite difficult to express in French, but once he understood, Michel found it very amusing.

One of Michel's *adjoints* phoned in the results to the counting centre for the *departement* and half an hour later the drinks were cleared away. Then everyone went home to watch the television news for the national results.

Alain, Pru and Mark joined Yves and Lucy at the château, and by ten-thirty a clear picture was emerging: Macron was in the lead with around twenty-four per cent of the votes, two per cent ahead of Le Pen. Fillon was a close third and the two left-wing candidates were out of the race.

That was how the final result was announced the next day. Macron would face Le Pen for the presidency in the second round run-off in a fortnight.

Three days later Mark received a call from Maitre Tournier.

"I think you may have caught a fish with a very bad smell, my friend," said the lawyer. "My contact at the tax office says that not everything seems to be in proper order at the association in which we are interested. The reporting and the account keeping seem to be deficient – if it exists at all – so now he is going to start leaning on Monsieur Suchet as the man stated to be responsible for its affairs. We make some progress now and I will call you again when I hear from him."

***

The media was preoccupied with the second round and the

two candidates.

Marine Le Pen had been in the news almost since childhood. In fact her father's ability to say anything he liked and get away with it had put the whole family in the spotlight for decades. Jean-Marie Le Pen, a deeply polarising figure then in his seventies, had come second in the first round of the 2002 presidential election before being trounced in the run-off, polling just eighteen per cent of the vote against eighty-two per cent for Jacques Chirac. Even then he had refused to give up on his political ambitions until he was thrown out of the party, the *Front National,* by his own daughter when she took over its presidency nine years later.

Emmanuel Macron was another matter entirely: only thirty-nine years of age at the time of the election, but, as Alain noted, a perfect candidate.

"Macron went to the right schools. If you want to be on the fast track in French politics you go to Sciences Po – he did and got a masters degree in public affairs – and then the *École National d'Administration*, followed by a senior job in the Inspectorate General of Finance."

Mark wanted to know if he ever had a real job.

"*Bien sûr*. He then joined Rothschilds as an investment banker."

Mark and Pru laughed, and she said, "No, we mean a real job where he actually met real people."

"Oh, I get it." Alain laughed. "*Desolé*, but no. In 2012 he joined President Hollande's staff, and was then given a junior ministry by Prime Minister Valls in 2014, from which he resigned in 2016 to form his own party, *En Marche!*, and stand for the presidency. Definitely no real job so far, and most of the people he has ever met have been politicians or civil servants."

"Sounds a bit like David Cameron to me," Mark grimaced.

"And the higher they fly the further they have to fall."

"Well, he is certainly high in the opinion polls at the moment, and about the only criticism of him is that he is married to a woman twenty years older than him. At least he's not gay, or we don't think he is. Most Frenchmen would hate that!"

After casting a postal vote to the district in Paris where he was registered, Alain returned to the *Mairie* with Mark on the seventh of May for the second round of voting. This time there was quite a crowd in attendance, but the set-up and polling procedures were essentially the same. They were greeted by Michel Ricard with a nod and a quick wave; the mayor was engaged on official business. Then they walked around the room, shaking hands and introducing themselves to those they didn't know.

The count was over by six thirty-five, due to a low turnout, which was perhaps unsurprising as the leader of the principal left-of-centre party had virtually told his supporters to boycott the election, deriding it as a sham contest between two right-wingers.

In Saint Audan, the vote was fifty-four per cent for Le Pen and forty-six for Macron. Alain looked at Mark and raised his eyebrows. "What did I tell you? In this neck of the woods they are conservative with a capital C."

This pattern, however, was not replicated throughout the nation. Le Pen won only two *departements*, both in the north. By early evening Macron was on his way to a landslide victory and Le Pen conceded. The final tally gave sixty-six per cent of the vote to him and thirty-four per cent to her.

"Well that's a relief," said Pru later over dinner. "It is interesting that the agricultural regions are so right-wing, but that's probably true for similar areas around the world. Look at Australia and the complete nut cases that get elected in

Queensland."

"Now we will see whether the voters support Macron at the elections for the Legislative Assembly in June and give him a government that will support his legislation," Alain pointed out. "Like all presidential candidates he has promised us a lot of reforms, but so often the winners have been unable to deliver because of a hostile parliament."

"That also resonates in Australia," said Mark. "Down there they have a habit of voting one party into office in the lower house and giving the Opposition the power in the Senate, their upper house. Guess you Frenchies are like that too – you just don't trust the blighters."

With little else to add on that topic they had a nightcap and hit the hay.

19.

REVELATIONS

PRU and Mark had only been back in England for a few days when Maitre Tournier rang.

"The fish you hooked is about to tell us everything," he said to Mark. "Monsieur Suchet wants to confess in return for a little sympathy. I have told him that sympathy is not mine to give. I am just, how do you say, a hired hack – I love that expression – but you perhaps might be more willing to give it. Anyway, he is coming to my office on Friday morning and will sign a written statement detailing the affairs of his association and his co-founder. Do you wish to be present?"

"*Maitre*, you are truly a magician," said Mark, "and presumably thanks also to your friend in the tax office?"

"Yes, you are right. My friendly tax officer has leaned on M. Suchet quite heavily. When he found out that Christian de Montfort might be involved he became especially active. Whether he does not agree with his politics, or for some more personal reason, I do not yet know. But it does not matter. We shall get Suchet's statement and my friend may get a little feather in his cap if he can bring on a prosecution. Can you be here, Mark? I don't want our little fish to panic and go to de Montfort for comfort."

"I'll be there, Louis, and I may bring Chris too if that's okay with you."

"*Naturellement,* it will be a pleasure to see you both. At ten in the morning then on Friday. *A vendredi.*"

At a quarter to ten on Friday morning Mark and Chris arrived at the office of Maitre Tournier and were seated with an expresso when Monsieur Suchet was announced. He turned down a coffee and asked for a glass of water. Tournier's assistant, a switched-on charmer in her mid-twenties, joined them to take notes, like Chris, and Tournier switched on a tape recorder before opening the meeting.

"Monsieur Suchet. You know these two *Messieurs* and you know also why they have a great interest in what you and your colleague have been trying to achieve, as it was you, posing as a Monsieur Demey, who went to the Château du Moulin and proposed to agree on a purchase price on behalf of an unnamed client. Let us start even earlier, when the LeBlanc family bought the neighbouring farm and received permission for a very unwelcome planning application. When you have finished that part of the story you can tell us about the art association for which you are the responsible person."

Suchet took a long drink of water and began to unfold the story.

"This all started ten years ago. Jean-Paul de Montfort had died, the château and the farmhouse were were falling into ruins, and nobody, neither Madame de Montfort nor Christian, had the money to pay off the huge mortgages, let alone dream of restoring the properties. Two banks had made the massive loans before the Great Financial Crash and neither wanted to admit to their senior management, much less their shareholders, that these loans were virtually unrecoverable. Lenders all over the world had this problem, but the French were even more reluctant to admit their failings. So the banks did a deal with Yvette, whereby the properties were separated from the loans, and optimistic valuations were placed on them. *Eh voila!* The problem was solved. And it was I who came up with that solution."

Suchet drew a deep breath and drank some more water before continuing.

"And that is when *my* problems began. Of course I discussed all this with Madame de Montfort and with Christian. Separately, you understand. When you, Monsieur Escott, came on the scene four years ago, Christian contacted me and told me of his plan and persuaded me to help him. Persuaded is perhaps not the right word – forced would be more correct. When I said I could not help him, he said that if I refused he would advise my directors and the media of what I had done. I had no choice. So I got my bank to maintain the loan on the farm, but transfer it into the names of LeBlanc and his wife. They paid nothing. In fact, no money changed hands. LeBlanc was in on the game because he is a silent partner in many of Christian's shady business deals. Then we drew up the planning application and took it to your mayor, Michel Ricard, who said he would wait until you had gone back to England and then put it before his *conseil municipal* for approval. He said its members never look at the applications, just tell him to sign and stamp them. Christian has many people prepared to do such things to help him."

Mark chipped in. "That sounds just like the way it happened."

"Christian is an evil man," Suchet declared. "Once he has you in his grasp he makes sure that you become ever more deeply committed. His next step with me was to form the association to whose meeting you came in February. It is entirely *bidon* –

phony – and was never intended to carry out the objectives in its documentation. But it has raised money from genuine donations and bought a few paintings, which are all hanging in Christian's house. It has also provided us with new cars and the ability to entertain some useful people in expensive restaurants, as well as allowing us to claim tax deductions on the donations we pretend to make. But Christian is clever: he never signs anything himself. He leaves all the dirty work to people like me so that he looks clean and I am totally compromised. If the man from the tax office takes a hard look at the association he will find a bank account, but no accounts or records showing where money has come from or how it has been spent. And no minutes, because there are no official meetings."

Suchet paused and looked down at his hands.

"But when it becomes public, people will say, 'I gave them money to set up this gallery of art in the Midi-Pyrenees. Where has it all gone?' And the person who most of them have met and received letters of thanks from is me."

Mark whistled. "That is some bloody scam."

"De Montfort is known for being devious, but no one has been able to prove his corruption," Suchet said. "Perhaps his luck is now running out. I think you have correctly guessed what we expected to happen. You and your family would be so horrified at the destruction of your peace and tranquillity that you would panic and sell at any price. When Christian got hold of both properties for a fraction of their real value, plus the planning authorisation, he would have several options, and all of them could make him a lot of money. He craves being a millionaire. But the thing that drove him the most, even more than money, was the determination to have his beloved château all to himself. The château that made him fight his mother and his brother with so much bitterness. The château they had all lost."

Chris responded. "Well, Monsieur Suchet, I am not legally qualified to give an opinion here in France, but if we were in England I would think that you are facing several years in prison. However, the person who has been the principal in the actions detrimental to our family is clearly de Montfort, and anything you can do to rid us of his malign presence will be greatly appreciated. What are the next steps, *Maitre*?"

"Thank you, Christopher," replied Maitre Tournier, using Chris's first name for the first time. "What Monsieur Suchet has told us will be turned into a written statement using his own words wherever possible, which he will sign. I would then recommend that he and I go to the police department for fiscal fraud, where Monsieur Suchet will offer himself for arrest. If you agree I will offer to represent him, and I think we shall be able to keep him out of jail if we can meet the bail conditions and he gives up his passport."

"I'd be happy to stand bail if it's not too heavy," Mark said.

When Mark and Chris got back to the château it looked to be at peace in the blazing sunshine. Alice had opened the windows, and curtains were billowing out from the first floor.

Mark addressed the household, declaring: "We are almost rid of him. We can start to relax again."

They decided to tell Michel Ricard about the meeting with Philippe Suchet, so Mark telephoned the *Mairie* and invited him over. Michel arrived in good spirits just after five o'clock and accepted a *pastis* and water. Mark took his usual scotch on the rocks and Chris opened a beer. They said *bon soirée* to Alice and settled down at the small table under the trees.

The mayor had no idea of the resolve that had now brewed into their ambush.

"Michel, we want you to know that we respect the good things you have done for the commune," Mark said. "You even married our Lucy. So we like you – despite the very bad things you have done to us. Now we are going to suggest the way you can start to put matters right again."

Michel could only stare into his glass as Mark went on.

"This morning we had a meeting at the office of our *avocat* with Philippe Suchet, who told us everything. He has made a written statement about his actions against us and the fiscal frauds carried out by the art association for which he is the designated person responsible. He is now talking to the police. Suchet explained why his actions were for the benefit of Christian de Montfort and how you were involved. We know from what we were told some time ago that you came under the influence of de Montfort because of the big favour his father did for your family during the war, and you have done everything he demanded ever since. That means you too are under his control – and that ends today."

"What do you mean?" said Michel, startled.

"I mean you will no longer accept instructions from Christian de Montfort, and from now on you will follow the instructions I am about to give you," Mark said, in a tone that brooked no dissension. "Firstly, I order you to call an emergency meeting of your *conseil municipale* at which I will be present with our *avocat*. Then you will tell your councillors what you have done to assist de Montfort throughout your time as mayor, and particularly in relation to the château. You will offer your resignation as mayor, which might not be accepted, but you will put it in writing anyway. We can discuss the details, but that is what we require you to do within the next twenty-four hours."

"And if I refuse?"

"I shall write to the *prefet* of this *departement* and the Minister for the Interior, setting out everything that has happened and specifically your role. We could probably, with the aid of the police and the tax department, uncover sufficient instances of fraud and deception over the years to merit a criminal case against you. We would also sue you for damages in respect to the costs and losses we have suffered. But if you accept, we shall not pursue you personally, although of course we cannot guarantee your immunity from investigation by the authorities."

Ricard sipped his *pastis* and contemplated his hands for more than a minute.

"I always feared this might happen, but perhaps it is better it happens now and not later. You know, I have been living in a nightmare for more than thirty years. At the start I had good thoughts and goals, but I have let them slip away. Once one makes the first really bad choice it goes like that. My saddest thoughts are about Adilah. When I met her I was in love. She was incredibly beautiful . . . and very young. We forged some papers so we could marry and she could come to France, and for a few years I think we were very happy. Then Christian met her and demanded that she become his mistress, or he would get her removed from France as an illegal immigrant.

"That was my first big mistake. I agreed to his demands and told Adilah she had to as well, and life in hell began. My loving relationship with Adilah was finished. She had a second child, a boy, and it was not mine. I believe de Montfort is the father. But we went on living together, as a family, and I have tried to be a father to Laurent. He is a delightful young man and I would be proud to have him as a real son. He knows none of this. Now he is I think happy to be with his mother and her new love, Antoine, who is a very nice man doing good things in his life. For me though, most things are finished. So I shall do what you have instructed, partly for my own sake, because I would like to do something good for what remains of my life. To you, Mark, and all your family, I give my apologies for the pain I have inflicted. But I also give you my thanks for bringing this matter – and for me this way of life – to a close. I shall leave now and call the meeting of the council for the day after tomorrow. Thank you again."

Mark and Chris smiled at each other as he walked away and had another drink, before snacking on some bread and cheese and hummus and smoked trout they found in the fridge. It had been an exhausting day, and they turned in early.

The full meeting of the *conseil municipale* took place as planned two days later and Maitre Tournier and Mark were in attendance. Chris had flown back to London to his day job.

As instructed, Michel Ricard put forward all the facts and owned up to his involvement with Christian de Montfort. A few councillors were stunned but most hardly looked surprised. There were no questions, and neither the *avocat* nor Mark had anything to add. Michel had said it all.

Michel's last act as mayor was reading out his resignation letter. His senior deputy, Lionel Cros, knew it was coming, thanked Michel for more than twenty years of service to the commune, and accepted his resignation on behalf of his fellow councillors, who all stood to applaud. Apart from a few formalities it was all over.

20.

ELECTIONS

WITH Emmanuel Macron in the Élysée Palace and his new party renamed *La Republique En Marche*, there was a scramble to find suitable candidates to contest the upcoming parliamentary elections. The president needed a National Assembly which would support his agenda and therefore planned to contest all five hundred and seventy-seven seats.

Now that most things between them were out in the open, Mark and Michel Ricard were occasionally enjoying each other's company again. Freed of his mayoral duties, Michel had more time for socialising. They were having a beer together one afternoon in beautiful late May sunshine when the conversation turned to voting.

"I think I'm beginning to get the hang of your electoral system," Mark said. "You have fewer constituencies than we do in the UK, but the big difference seems to me that in a general election we have a first-past-the-post system, which means the candidates with the most votes win. In France you have two rounds of voting. Can you explain to me how it works?"

"It's not that complicated, Mark. To win a seat in round one, a candidate has to achieve an absolute majority as well as at least twenty-five per cent of the votes in their own constituency. This rarely happens because there are so many candidates from different parties, and in the first round some voters will choose someone who cannot win, as a sort of protest. As you will see, some extreme left or right candidates may do quite well, but if they qualify, their votes in the second round may actually fall. Come to the vote counting on the eleventh of June, and now that I am no longer mayor I can spend some time with you and point out these things."

On voting day, Macron's LREM Party ended up fielding more than five hundred candidates. An *Autan* was whipping up from the south and the skies were an ominous grey, but this could not have been the only reason for the record low turnout: nationally, just forty-eight per cent of eligible voters. In the constituency containing Saint Audan it was just over fifty per cent. While every local candidate attracted votes, none had enough to be elected outright and only five qualified to go through to the second round. Christian de Montfort was one, finishing third behind candidates representing Macron's LREM and *Le Front National*, the party of Marine Le Pen.

"Why would someone stand for a party that only received three votes, as one did here?" Mark asked as he watched electoral officials doing the tally in the *Mairie*. "Presumably there is some sort of registration fee for candidates."

"There is," Michel said, "and it should be a lot higher. But you see, we French still cling to the idea that everyone should be able to express their view and offer themselves for election, so the cost is low."

"Ah yes, liberty, equality, fraternity and all that."

"*Oui!* Precisely. I must say that today's result does not look good for de Montfort or the Republicans generally. I think we should expect some big upsets in the next round."

The second round of voting took place a week later, on the eighteenth of June, and Mark and Michel were back at the *Mairie* just before the polls closed. The number of votes cast was down even further on the previous week's all-time low, making Michel surmise that a lot of people thought the result was already decided.

"A foregone conclusion, we would probably say," Mark put it.

"Exactly, and I will remember that expression, *mon ami*. We shrug our shoulders and turn up the palms of our hands, very French gestures, when we think there is nothing we can do to alter events. '*Que sera sera*.' And you will have noticed that, as we expected, the votes for Macron and Le Pen's parties have increased, but the rest have either stayed the same or decreased. Shall we stay here for the final count of the whole constituency? There is a screen to receive a broadcast directly from constituency headquarters where all the votes will be counted and the results will be announced. We can buy a drink, as long as you only want beer or *pastis.*"

Over the next few hours Mark had several beers and tucked into baguettes filled with local produce to keep the effects of the alcohol in check. He phoned Pru and offered to bring her to the *Mairie*, but she was watching the election coverage on TV and having dinner. Mark bought his third baguette as the new mayor came over and poured him another drink.

At ten o'clock the TV coverage switched to the main tally room. The local host was explaining the progress with collating the votes, which had first been phoned in and then verified against the tally sheets Mark had watched the scrutineers filling in.

"*Mesdames et Messieurs*, I will now invite our five candidates to come up on the stage, and in a minute or so I shall read out the results and we can acclaim the elected member for this constituency," the host said.

Two women stepped forward, followed by three men. They all looked deadly serious, but one, a youngish woman, could barely suppress a smile, while Christian de Montfort looked as if he had been forced to swallow sour milk. He took the last chair.

The host was handed a sheet of paper and read out the vote count for each candidate, before declaring that Madame Marguerite Bonfon was elected to the *Assemblée National*.

All five candidates rose from their chairs and three clustered around the newly elected member, shaking her hand and congratulating her. De Montfort turned his back on them and walked out through the wings. He had been defeated in the seat he held for twenty years by more than five thousand votes – by a political novice on the Macron bandwagon.

21.

A SAD LOSS

LIKE the French voters, everybody at the château breathed a sigh of relief when the elections were over and a new government was sworn in. Now it was summertime, the schools had broken up, and every weekend there were reports of huge traffic jams as cars ferried vacationers to and from holiday resorts.

With the château theirs to enjoy, freed of the threat from Christian de Montfort after nearly two years of worry, neither the Escotts nor the Burlingtons hankered after getaways on an overcrowded beach. But sometimes Chris and his family would take off for a few days and head down to the Med, on the coast near Perpignan or just over the Spanish border, where Chloe and Joey could paddle in the surf and build sand castles as their grandparents had a break.

The "house full" sign would soon be going up. Mark and Pru had invited her parents to stay for as long as they wanted, and although the OB was showing signs of ageing they were there like a shot. Toby and Jenny also planned to spend the month of August at the château, along with Sarah and Tom, who now had two little ones. Then there was Lucy and Yves, who had decided to close the restaurant for two weeks and were now full-time residents.

Alice, who didn't have a family, enjoyed being kept busy with the cooking and housekeeping. As for the garden and the park, Toby enjoyed driving the ride-on motor mower once in a while to keep the grass neat.

Towards the end of the month Mark received a call from another *notaire*, who said he represented the late Yvette de Montfort.

"The late?" said Mark, shocked.

"Yes. She died of a heart attack two days ago and there is some urgency in arranging her *obseques*. Monsieur Escott, I have a rather unusual request to make of you, and you must not hesitate to say no if you are not happy with it."

"Please, go ahead."

"Thank you. Madame de Montfort left amongst her papers a request as to how and where she wished to be interred, and I have made arrangements for the funeral service at L'Eglise de Saint Jean Le Baptiste in Saint Audan at eleven hours, in two days' time. This will be followed by her interment in the de Montfort family tomb in the church yard. I have the permission of the parish priest for this, but I can find nobody in the family with whom to discuss these plans."

"Where do I fit in?"

"It is not you personally, *Monsieur*, although the late lady had a very high regard for you, so much as the château. Madame de Montfort said the best years of her life were spent there and she would like to make her final journey from the château to the church. This would mean bringing her coffin to the château and allowing the cars forming the *cortège* to park there for a short time. But there is one more thing. Madame de Montfort asked me to read her last testament and has left me a list – a very short one, I must say – of the people she would like to be present. You and your wife are two, naturally, but she has another favour to ask of you. She would like the testament to be read out inside the château, after the interment."

Mark asked for a moment to think about the requests.

"Well, to start with, we shall all be very sad at this loss," he told the *notaire*. "We did not know Yvette very well or for very long, but we found her to be most gracious and not at all antagonistic towards us when we were buying and then moving into the château. Indeed she seemed very happy that we had managed to restore some of its former glory, and we were very sad for her when she was forced to leave the farmhouse. I'm sure my wife and I and our other family members who are co-owners of the château will be happy to say yes to her requests. But could you tell me who are the others she wished to have present?"

"Of course, and thank you, Monsieur Escott. I have not invited any of them yet, as I need your answer first. The list is not long. It starts with her surviving son Christian and his wife Suzanne, but I have been unable to contact them. There is Madame Adilah Ricard, who will sing during the service, and her husband, as well as the man I understand to now be her partner, Doctor Lefevre. Also the new mayor and his wife, and six people from this commune who were of help to Madame de Montfort at one time or another. So, including you, your brother-in-law and your wives, if everyone comes who is invited, we shall be just over a dozen or so."

"That will be no problem," said Mark.

The *notaire* thanked Mark again and promised to try to contact the others immediately and send him a list of acceptances the following evening. When he left, Mark asked Toby, their wives, the OB and Lady Ann to join him for a drink as he broke the sad news. It was only five-thirty but he needed one.

***

On the morning of the funeral it was hot and getting hotter. Alice put cold drinks out as well as light refreshments for those returning after the church service. The hearse arrived at ten-thirty. Mark had told the *notaire* the coffin could be brought into the château, but he declined, saying, "I'm sure *Madame* is happy just knowing that her last journey starts from here."

The cars in the cortège took Adilah and Antoine, Michel Ricard, the new mayor and his wife and Mark's family, but there was no sign of the de Montforts. At five minutes to the hour the *notaire* gave a signal to the funeral director and the vehicles left the château on the slow drive, following the hearse down the lanes and up the hill to the Catholic church.

The lady organist was playing softly when they walked in, and the flowers and wreaths that Mark and the *notaire* ordered brought colour to the service without overdoing it. Four sturdy young men got out of a black sedan and one opened the rear door of the hearse. They slid the coffin out, hefted it onto their shoulders, and followed the funeral director and about thirty mourners into the nave.

The organ stopped, and upon reaching the altar the pallbearers placed the casket on twin trestles as the funeral director laid a wreath of white flowers on top of it. At this moment another couple walked into the church – Christian de Montfort and his wife, who sat in the front pew.

Christian had aged badly in the months since losing the election. He needed a haircut and a shave, but the most striking changes were in his posture, normally so erect and dominating, now with sagging shoulders and lowered head, and his face, prematurely lined and gaunt. The eyes that once glittered (like a snake's, Mark had often remarked) were dull and lifeless.

The service commenced with a prayer before the priest invited Michel Ricard to come forward and deliver the eulogy. The *notaire* had asked him to officiate after getting no response from Christian.

"Thank you, father. *Mesdames et Messieurs,* friends and family of Yvette. Thank you for coming here today to celebrate the life of a woman who spent most of her adult years in our community of Saint Audan. I was only two when she married Xavier, but even as a child I was always aware of her, partly I suppose because of the château in which she lived, which we all aspired to visit. And partly because the lives of the de Montforts were constantly discussed. They were the *célèbres* of our little commune. I knew her sons of course, who were a bit older than me, and I am glad to see Christian with us today. I didn't really get to know Yvette well until I was about fifteen, when she asked my parents if I could help her with an event to raise funds for this church. After that it was always my great pleasure to spend time with her and Xavier, who was responsible for my early interest in local politics.

"But it is to Yvette that I owe the most, my love of books to start with. I could read, but Yvette taught me what to read and how to enjoy reading. She encouraged me to go to a business school where I learned about marketing and finance, which can be useful even for a farmer. She showed me that working with other people to help those who are less well advantaged could be most rewarding, and I am happy to be doing that again. And when I fell in love" – here he turned towards Adilah, who was sitting near the organist – "it was Yvette who encouraged me to marry my love and find more happiness, which, sadly, I was so stupid as to throw away." Michel paused in reflection, then went on to finish the eulogy. "We should remember that Yvette was a wonderful citizen during the five decades she lived in our commune. She promoted and protected so many things we now take for granted, such as the home for the elderly, our community centre and the day care centre. Certainly Yvette was not always working alone, but she was always our guiding star. Thank you, Yvette, and God bless you."

As Michel sat down several people were weeping. The organist played the first notes of a popular hymn and Adilah's voice swelled through the little church. The congregation joined in, then the priest said more prayers, another hymn followed, and the mourners filed up to the altar to receive holy communion. After the final hymn the priest waved his incense burner over the coffin as he intoned the last blessing:

Le Seigneur soit avec vous.
    Réponse: Et avec votre esprit.
Que Dieu tout-puissant vous bénisse
    Le Père; le Fils et le Saint-Esprit.
Réponse: Amen.
Allez dans la paix du Christ.
Réponse: Nous rendons grace à Dieu.

The priest led the mourners out of the church and down the hill to the cemetery, where the pallbearers placed Yvette's casket inside the de Montfort family mausoleum which was more than a hundred years old. The earliest inscriptions of the ancestors were fading away, in contrast to the later ones dedicated to the memory of Xavier and his first son, Jean-Paul. As he shook the incense from his thurible, the priest blessed the tomb and Yvette was lowered to her final resting place.

22.

THE LAST TESTAMENT

FIFTEEN minutes later, those invited to attend the reading of Yvette's testament were being welcomed into the hall in the château, where sixteen chairs had been placed around four trestle tables forming a square. The guests were offered soft drink, but Christian asked if wine was available. Mark nodded and Alice fetched a bottle of Gaillac red. Christian swallowed a full glass and sat down, looking even worse than he did in church.

The *notaire* opened the proceedings.

"*Mesdames et Messieurs*, thank you for coming and for fulfilling the late Madame de Montfort's final wish. She left a last testament that she wished me to read to you all, which I will now do."

Dear friends. After a fairly long and often happy life I have come to its end. You have all played some part in it, and I am glad of this final opportunity to thank those of you who have shown me love and friendship, and to also tell everyone some of the things I have learned. I have very little to leave in terms of money or possessions but for a few small tokens, which I shall come to.

Prudence and Mark Escott. From the moment I met you I felt your warmth and sympathy, and also that of Jenny and Toby Burlington. Yours is a remarkable family, and much of that quality must come from Sir Robert and Lady Ann whom I hardly know. Thank you for everything and for always making me feel welcome at the château, including this the last time.

Adilah and Michel. You have been two of the steady rocks to which I have anchored my life on many occasions. Adilah, your love and affection has been steadfast over many years and certainly since the death of Jean-Paul. You were a constant companion when I was most in need, and to you I am leaving my black opal necklace and my deep love. I wish a long and happy life to you and your new partner, a kind and trustworthy man who has also been of great help to me. Thank you, Docteur Lefevre.

Michel. You have often felt like a third son to me, and I thank you for all the help and attention you have given me over so many years. I have nothing tangible to give you, so a small piece of advice will have to be sufficient. Always think carefully of the consequences of your choices. I was very sad when I saw you taking some wrong decisions, but now you seem to be starting a new way of living and I am happy again for you. Please accept my love and good wishes.

The *notaire* continued to read the will, which acknowledged and left small gifts to a few other people who had been important to Yvette, including a housekeeper and a gardener and her working companions in the community. Finally she came to her family.

Xavier was the best thing to happen in my life. We shared so many things, including the tragedy of his first wife's death. In her last months he was almost broken and I comforted him. Not in any sexual way. He was always very respectful and I was very young. But when that was over and he was recovering we started to enjoy each other's company, and that led to love and marriage.

Xavier was a man with two personalities. With me and the boys he was always kind and gentle, and encouraged us to help out in the commune. He often spoke of his father, who had been a dedicated supporter of Toulouse and a councillor of that city in the 19th century. But Xavier also had another side. As a younger man he admitted to lusting after power, not for any specific reward, just to know he had it. During the war his position was enormously powerful, but in the circumstances it made him incredibly vulnerable, and the greater his power, the greater was his vulnerability. This happened when he chose to accept the political position offered to him by Maréchal Pétain, his old commanding officer.

Once in that position he had to go forward. He told me that he managed to do many good things for France – getting supplies to our prisoners of war in Germany was one. But he also admitted to me in moments of intimacy that he had supported the German cause, and, it is terrible to say, Hitler's Final Solution.

There was a gasp of astonishment from the assembled mourners, but the notaire continued.

Xavier created secret accounts funded by the government, as well as corporations and individuals, to pay for the Milice in their rounding-up of the Jews from 1942 onwards – the shame of les grands rafles. After the war, he told me he was very lucky that evidence of these appalling acts was not brought out at his trial, but by 1946 the "old guard" were largely back in charge, and the last thing they wanted was for people of his wartime status to be found guilty of collaboration with the Germans. So he was acquitted, but many people knew the truth.

Our sons inherited their father's two personalities: Jean-Paul the kind and gentle one, and Christian the one lusting for power. Christian, if you are listening to this, I want you to know that I always loved you, but I have not liked you since you were a little boy. You ruined the life of your brother, you deeply saddened me, and you spoiled the lives of many in your pursuit of power. I have nothing to offer you except the words of Our Lord: "Repent, for the Kingdom of Heaven is at hand."

And now I am at peace.

The notaire lowered his papers and looked around. All eyes were on Christian, who rose to his feet, glaring.

"So now you know almost everything . . . everything I have lost. You filthy English," he spat at Mark, "have taken my château and my money. I have spent two days and a night being interrogated by the police, and now I am facing charges of fraud and money-laundering and could get five years in prison. I have lost my seat in the National Assembly. I have lost my father, my brother, my mother. And now she has accused my father of supporting the extermination of the Jews! There is just one person left to me, but he does not yet know I am his father. Yes," he yelled in defiance, "I have a son to carry on my name!"

Adilah spoke in a low but clear voice. "No you don't. Laurent is not your son."

Christian fixed her with a hateful stare.

"You lie, you whore! You are a liar! You told me that it was my child when you became pregnant and again after he was born."

"Yes, I was your whore then, and it was easier for me to go along with the pretence. But I had all the tests done, and Laurent has another man as his father. It is proven. It is not you – it is Antoine."

Suzanne de Montfort rarely spoke, but now she attacked her husband with unbridled venom.

"Yes, we all lied to you, Christian, it was the only way we could live with you. When I could not conceive, you insisted that I have all the tests because you kept saying it was my fault. No problems were found with me, I was fertile. But would you get checked out? Certainly not! So I secretly took some of your sperm and had it tested. And do know what? The English have an expression for it. You were firing blanks, Christian. Pop, pop! Your sperm is just like you, it is no good. You are worth less than nothing, because you are a fraud and an adulterer. You have never had a child and you never will have a child. And yes, you have lost everything, and that now includes me!"

Suzanne pushed her chair back and stormed out.

As Christian stood there, unable to respond, the lines multiplying on his face seemed to splinter into a thousand particles. He put his hands over his eyes as if he were about to cry, but emitted a high-pitched keening sound like an animal in agony, turned, and stumbled out of the room, out of the château, and out of their lives.

The château watched his dramatic departure and was pleased.

23.

LOOKING FORWARD

AS SUMMER drew to a close the family was enjoying the last of the sunshine and the release from such a sustained period of tension.

"Well, we can't say we haven't had some experiences over the past few years," said Toby as they sat outside having a drink in the cooling evening. "Tough going at times but well worth it, mostly thanks to you, Mark. You pulled us through the worst and now we can relax and enjoy ourselves."

"It wasn't just me, Toby. I had the backing of you lot and more than a few friends here in France. We were lucky there, and also having the resources to fight. Without the money for a legal stoush and everything else it would have been a lot worse. I heard this morning that the LeBlancs are moving out next week and the farmhouse will be back on the market. Think we should buy it?"

"No bloody way, for the same reasons as last time," Pru insisted. "The château is enough responsibility, and when the *conseil municipal* revokes the planning authorisation at its next meeting, which Lionel says they will, that danger should be gone forever."

Adilah and Antoine dropped by with their son, full of happiness after explaining everything to Laurent.

"We are so pleased for you," Jenny told them.

Laurent, now a good-looking young man of nineteen, spoke up.

"For me it was both a shock and a wonderful surprise when they told me, but I had been noticing that I did not have much in common with the man I thought was my father. And although I respected the way he behaved with me and my sister, it hurt me the way he treated my mother. Now I have been to see him, and I told him that I still love him despite everything that has happened, and I think we shall always be good friends. And the most important part for me is that *Maman* is so happy. As for my real father," he beamed, putting his arm round Antoine's shoulders, "well, what is there to say? A really bad man, *n'est-ce pas?* Getting his patients in the family way!"

They chuckled, and Antoine looked abashed before he grinned.

"Let's move on from my misdeeds, for which I'm now paying. Tell them what you are planning, Laurent," he said.

"Well, I have finished my first year at the University of Toulouse in the faculty of medicine at Rangueil and passed the exam, so all I have now is eight more years of study and I will be a doctor like my father."

Toby was stunned. "Nine years of study to be a doctor? That is amazing. No wonder the health service in France is so good."

"Yes, and there are additional courses for various specialities after that if I wish. But I just want to get qualified. I must tell you that Antoine has been amazingly supportive, and I'm afraid that when I am home we speak of medicine all the time. It must be rather boring for *Maman, non*?"

Adilah's eyes were shining with pride as he spoke.

"I am just so happy for all of us," she said. "You must know that except for those first few years with Michel I have never known such *joie de vivre*. And speaking of Michel, we have all become good friends again and he is going to start voluntary work soon in one of the departments at Laurent's medical school."

***

Nine months later Lucy had a baby boy and they named him Paul, because the name was the same in English and French. He was born in the château with the help of a lovely *sage femme*, a local midwife, because his parents were so attached to the place that they felt they could not give their first child a better start in life. They also decided that they would no longer make the forty-minute trip to and from the restaurant each day, so with Eloise's approval they converted the floor above it into a two-bedroom apartment and moved in. After a few weeks off work, with Emile filling in, Lucy was back at reception, keeping an eye on the baby via a video unit hooked up to his crib.

La Table Aux Platanes was booming. Yves proved to be an excellent restaurateur, garnering a second Michelin star and maintaining patronage and profitability by keeping the high standard of food up and the prices down to cater primarily for the locals. The business also benefited from Lucy and Yves' popularity among the regulars, who opened their hearts to a couple blessed by love and good fortune.

Mark disposed of his last remaining business assets and went into virtual retirement a few months shy of turning sixty. Owning the château and moving to France was a dream come true, but he wondered what he was going to do all day.

When they moved permanently to Saint Audan, Pru enrolled in a conversion course at the University of Montpellier to earn the qualification that would allow her to practice in France as a music therapist. Then she went into business with three younger therapists, and Mark leased, renovated and equipped commercial space near the centre of Toulouse where they set up two soundproofed studios and an office.

Pru was energised by this reconnection to her vocational passion, bringing the joy of music to the unfortunate ones who all too often were shunned by society because they were not "normal". But times were beginning to change, and she and her colleagues found a growing demand for their services as the French rethought their attitudes towards handicapped children, especially those on the autism spectrum who were at last being offered proper support.

One of Pru's first clients was Mathilde, now an eight-year-old girl with bundles of energy who loved working with her on the piano. Her ability and wish to communicate was improving immensely, but she still needed a lot of attention – and found it in a new school which provided trained staff to help children with special needs.

Unlike Pru, however, Jenny decided to retire, worn down by the pressures of her job and incessant demands from the parents of children with special needs.

"I've had enough," she said to Toby the day she decided to give it away. "My department is supposed to find new schools willing to take on kids who've been excluded by other schools. One of my cases is a harmless fifteen-year-old boy who was in trouble for bringing a firearm into class and showing it around. The teacher confiscated it and put him in isolation, which was the correct procedure, and the principal phoned the boy's mother to come in. She said the gun – which unfortunately was loaded – was a birthday present from his cousin who lived on a farm, and she could see nothing wrong with his behaviour. Or hers, come to that. Where the hell am I going to find a school prepared to take a kid like him with a parent like that?"

Parents, in Jenny's view, had little respect for teachers or their rights. "Teachers in schools around our part of London are leaving in droves and there just aren't enough new ones coming in to replace them. In five years' time there will be a crisis."

While Jenny didn't miss her job or her salary – Toby earned more than enough to keep them comfortable – she did want to do something productive and keep busy. So she learned how to communicate with the profoundly deaf by sign language, and volunteered her services to a school that specialised in teaching these students, as well as their classmates with other learning difficulties. "ENABLE" was the school's motto, and Jenny embraced it wholeheartedly because she was an enabler in the best sense of the word: a generous woman who wanted to do something positive for those less fortunate.

Toby stayed in touch with Alain Frugier and they caught up regularly at the same coffee shop near the British Museum where their paths first crossed. Last time they met, Toby found the historian sitting out on the pavement under a sun umbrella, reading a very heavy-looking book.

"It's a new one about General de Gaulle – and it's written by an Englishman," Alain said after they shook hands. "I must say it's very interesting, with several new slants on the man who either saved France twice or was the cause of much that is wrong with France today, according to one's point of view."

"Well, we Brits mostly think of him as one of the best things your country ever produced," said Toby with a smile. "But we've also read that he didn't get on with Churchill or Eisenhower, let alone Stalin. In fact he seemed to make a point of upsetting them. A very difficult personality, wouldn't you say?"

"It was the same with his countrymen," Alain conceded. "Most people had never heard of him until he started his wartime broadcasts from London, and then many feared that he was preparing France for an Allied invasion, which actually worried them, so they were against what he was preaching. And then in 1945 he became France's national hero for saving us all from *les sales Boches*. But what he did after being re-elected president in 1958 is probably the main thing the French people have against de Gaulle. He gave away Algeria and he has never been forgiven for that by a big part of the population."

"You French seem to love strong men on the one hand but spend your time undermining them."

"You are correct, my friend. We love democracy but we fear the consequences. Democracy is Greek for rule by the people, which can mean direct democracy, where the citizens as a whole form a government body and vote directly on each issue – Switzerland almost does that – or representative democracy, where the citizens elect representatives, which is what we do. But then, of course, we distrust them. When we elected Macron it was for change. Now we don't want what he is proposing. We live by the myth of the Glorious Revolution, yet we are one of the most conservative races on earth."

"Still love it though," said Toby. "No other country has so many cheeses."

"And now you are, I think the expression is, pulling my leg, Toby. But you are again correct. We French love diversity in everything, and we excel at research and experimentation. No other country has won so many Nobel Prizes for breakthroughs in medical research, and we contribute to many fields of science. And at the moment our Airbus is the world market leader with the airlines."

"Well, let's hope France can hold things together over the next few years, Alain, because my instincts tell me we're all in for a very rocky ride."

And Toby was not far wrong.

***

As the winter petered out, Mark and Pru were having a mid-morning coffee in the main room of the château, on a pleasant, warm day that gave promise of a lovely spring.

A text message from Toby pinged on Mark's iPhone: SELL SELL SELL!!! Mark took his brother-in-law's advice and immediately rang his stockbroker, just in time to come out of the crash that Toby had been predicting almost unscathed. But the economic fallout for millions of people, especially those approaching retirement, was devastating. Worldwide, a number of banks closed their doors and froze hundreds of thousands of deposit accounts. This time, unlike the Great Financial Crisis of 2007-08, the banks were not considered to be "too big to fail". They were just "too big" – and some of the biggest did fail, crashing through the global economy like dominoes.

Mark and Toby had followed the safety precautions long attributed to the French peasantry and kept some tidy sums of cash "under the mattress". Though weathering the storm, even they had to cut their cloth and start economising. When the financial nuclear bomb went off, the Burlingtons moved into the cosy millhouse beside the château, to live with the Escotts. Both pledged to do whatever they could to support their children, who were buffeted in the aftermath. And every day, these escapees from England thanked their lucky stars that they had found their haven for retirement in France.

Lady Ann and the Old Bastard joined the others at the

château early in the summer. The OB was slowing almost to a stop, but he still had plenty to say about the world in general and politicians in particular.

"Don't bloody well know what the universe is coming to," he would rail. "You'd think we could find some leaders with brains as well as balls . . . perhaps even a return of the Margaret of Blessed Memory." But no one was too optimistic.

The reborn château had grown used to the steady influx and departure of the owners and their guests. It could sense their enjoyment, the free spirit of the youngsters, the peace of mind of the seniors – proof that it was perfectly serving its intended purpose.

As it gazed upon the contented English family sitting in the garden under the shady trees day after day, enjoying their drinks and their lively discourse, the château smiled to itself. It had been there for centuries before them and it would be there long after they were gone. But for now, the magnificent old country manor was very, very satisfied to be owned by such nice people – even if they were foreigners.

THANKS

Thank you to my publisher and friend Philip Walker, and editor extraordinary Gary Martin. Many thanks to Philip Mortlock, Amber Quin, Nick Young and everyone at Origin.